KEYS TO BEING SET FREE

OVERCOMING HANG-UPS AND
ADDICTIONS

KEYS TO BEING SET FREE

OVERCOMING HANG-UPS AND
ADDICTIONS

Pete Robertson

Set Free Press

First Printing, 2023

Printed in the United States of America

To Order Additional copies of this resource, you may order online at www.setfreepress.com.

Unless indicated otherwise, Scripture quotations are taken from the Holy Bible, English Standard Version, Copyright The Holy Bible, English Standard Version® (ESV®) Copyright © 2001 by Crossway, a publishing ministry of Good News Publishers. All rights reserved worldwide. Used by permission.

ISBN/SKU 979-8-218-96060-5
EISBN 979-8-8689-7554-7

A Ministry of Natural Discipleship
10524 Moss Park Rd 204-339
Orlando FL 32832

CONTENTS

BEFORE YOU START

Will the Natural Discipleship "Keys to Being Set Free" curriculum be right for you? Read this introduction, answer each question, and decide whether you should proceed with the "Keys to Being Set Free". If so, let your Coach know and set up a time to meet and get started on this amazing journey of freedom.

Natural Discipleship's "Keys to Being Set Free" curriculum is a biblically balanced curriculum that will assist in bringing long-term healing to your hurts, addictions, and hang-ups. The majority of individuals who are a part of the "Keys to Being Set Free" family are followers of Christ who desire spiritual revival in their personal lives. The reality is that we all have hang-ups and or addictions in various forms. People associated with Keys to Being Set Free comprehend that there are aspects of their lives that require improvement. They display humility and some of them are in desperate need of a complete transformation.

What is a hang-up? A hang-up is any bad habit or thing we do that is not in accordance with God's perfect will. We acquire these hangups while trying to alleviate our life's struggles and find meaning in our purpose and identity. As we repair ourselves and broken relationships, it will lead us to new healthy truths and life-giving habits. "Keys to Being Set Free" may be the natural next step you take yourself and your disciple through.

Natural Discipleship "Keys to Being Set Free" can assist you in finding Freedom

Keys to Being Set Free curriculum is intended to offer you the tools you need to lead the triumphant and abundant life that Christ came to give you. The optimal atmosphere for this is one-on-one where you and your leader can be open and vulnerable to one another.

This curriculum is designed to support the growth of discipleship and works alongside social group gatherings such as Celebrate Recovery, AA meetings, Church of the Highlands Freedom Groups, Teen Challenge, and Freedom in Christ, among others. If you are already involved in one of these ministries, there is no need for you to stop attending your group. This particular setting is intended for one-on-one conversations rather than a group dynamic.

Although there may be some similarities in the curriculum, we have found that the individualized approach focused on discipleship multiplication helps individuals discover their personal calling while experiencing freedom. If you are not part of any of these group ministries, that is perfectly fine as well. It is not necessary to be involved in order to fulfill the great commission. Our main goal is to advance the kingdom of God and help you grow your relationship with the Lord. We also aim to address any areas of your life that may have led to poor decision-making in the past.

It is important to note that certain individuals may require additional assistance from a trained Christian psychologist after completing each "KEY" in this curriculum. If you fall into this category, we strongly recommend seeking the assistance of a psychologist who has a biblical perspective and can guide you in working through any challenging issues you may be facing.

Every disciple of Jesus has a unique story, and some have witnessed and experienced things that no one should ever have to go through. Some have been in terrible relationships that have seriously harmed their life. Others have been extremely selfish in their life choices, causing many bridges to be burned along the way. Whatever your story is, I guarantee you that there is victory over the heaviness that has weighed you down in Jesus. If you are a Christian who believes you don't have many issues and that your relationship with God is going well, this curriculum is for you as well. As you progress through each key, you will discover areas in your life that you were unaware existed. God can and will strategically point out ways for you to draw ever closer to Him. This curriculum is intended for everyone including Pastors, and mature and new Christians alike.

Let's face it, we live in a damaged world, we all cope with the pains, hardships, and routines of daily life. We believe that no one is capable of or should seek to confront their hang-ups and pains on their own. "Keys to Being Set Free" is an awesome one-on-one community of strugglers who bravely enter a safe and beautiful area to be open and honest about their sorrow and the negative ways they perceive themselves, God, and others. In this process, we come to understand that some of the behaviors we may have created to escape our sorrow have brought problems to our lives and the lives of those closest to us.

First, let's be honest with ourselves, spend a moment going over "The hang-up or addiction symptoms list" below, and truthfully confess out loud if you are struggling with any of these areas:

The hang-up or addiction symptoms List:

Outburst of Anger, Bitterness, Unforgiveness, Self-Protection, Codependency, Drug Addiction, Alcoholism, Eating Disorder, Food obsessions (such as when the stresses of life cause a desire for comfort food), Sexual Porn, Gambling Addiction, Depressed often, having low self-esteem, Love and Relationship Addiction (such as a current toxic relationship or a revolving door of bad relationships), Parent problems, Grief from past heartache, Mobile phone/Social Media Addiction, Childhood Dysfunction, Problems with Money or Lack of Money, Physical abuse, Sexual and or emotional abuse, Playing video Games Addiction, Working out Addiction, Workaholic Addiction, Mental health problems, Regret and Shame, Victim mentality.

Q1. What hang-ups or hurts are you currently dealing with? (If you're still not sure, that's ok, this curriculum can still help you discover some you were not aware of and draw you closer to God)

(Spend time discussing with your coach your hang-ups and addictions, and how they have been or are currently affecting your life. Be honest with each other, remove the facades, and humble yourself.)

KEY AREAS WE WILL FOCUS ON TO HELP YOU OVERCOME HANG-UPS AND ADDICTIONS

To achieve genuine freedom, we need to adopt a lifestyle that replicates itself and expands our commitment to the Great Commandment (Matt 22:34-40) and Great Commission (Matt 28:16-20). Your personal journey towards freedom will create a movement that is **God guides, is reliant on the Holy Spirit, centered on the Bible, focused on obedience, based on discovery, driven by discipleship, and obsessed with multiplication.** You will experience true freedom when you learn these habits while actively discipling others and witnessing them doing the same.

Guided by God

"Go therefore and make disciples of all nations, baptizing them in the name of the Father and of the Son and of the Holy Spirit, teaching them to observe all that I have commanded you. And behold, I am with you always, to the end of the age." Mathew 28:19-20

Reliant on the Holy Spirit

"And hope does not put us to shame, because God's love has been poured out into our hearts through the Holy Spirit, who has been given to us." Romans 5:5

"And do not get drunk with wine, for that is debauchery, but be filled with the Spirit" Ephesians 5:8

Centered on the Bible

"All Scripture is breathed out by God and profitable for teaching, for reproof, for correction, and for training in righteousness, that the man of God may be complete, equipped for every good work." 2 Timothy 3:16-18

Focused on Obedience

"And this is love: that we walk in obedience to his commands. As you have heard from the beginning, his command is that you walk in love." 2 John 1:6

Based on Discovery

"No one can come to me unless the Father who sent me draws him. And I will raise him up on the last day. It is written in the Prophets, 'And they will all be taught by God.' Everyone who has heard and learned from the Father comes to me— not that anyone has seen the Father except he who is from God; he has seen the Father." John 6:44-46

Driven by Discipleship

"From now on, therefore, we regard no one according to the flesh. Even though we once regarded Christ according to the flesh, we regard him thus no longer. Therefore, if anyone is in Christ, he is a new creation. The old has passed away; behold, the new has come. All this is from God, who through Christ reconciled us to himself and gave us the ministry of reconciliation; that is, in Christ God was reconciling the world to himself, not counting their trespasses against them, and entrusting to us the message of reconciliation.

Therefore, we are ambassadors for Christ, God making his appeal through us. We implore you on behalf of Christ, be reconciled to God. For our sake he made him to be sin who knew no sin, so that in him we might become the righteousness of God." 2 Corinthians 5:16-21

Obsessed with Multiplication

"What you have heard from me in the presence of many witnesses entrust to faithful men, who will be able to teach others also." 2 Timothy 2:2

Q2. What does it mean to achieve genuine freedom according to the provided statements above?

Q3. What roles do God, the Holy Spirit, the Bible, obedience, discovery, discipleship, and multiplication play in this process?

LIVING OUT THE "TREE OF LIFE" AND LEARNING THE DIFFERENCE

We will learn how to admit we are powerless over our hurts and hang-ups through the "Tree of Life" outlined in Gen 2:8-9. *Romans 7:18 "For I know that good itself does not dwell in me, that is, in my sinful nature. For I have the desire to do what is good, but cannot carry it out."*

To admit we are powerless is the start of opening up our understanding of how God can help us. God desires that we know Him intimately and live in our true identity as His children.

You will discover what it means to live in the "Tree of Life" and how a simple yet profound shift in viewpoint will affect every aspect of your life.

Q4. Are you ready to admit that you are powerless over your sin and need God's help?

LEARNING HOW TO FOLLOW THE SPIRIT IN A DEEPER WAY

The Bible speaks of the Spirit-filled life, but it often feels difficult to attain. Through Being Set Free, you will understand the spiritual order of principles and the importance of nourishing your spirit above your emotions and flesh for a Spirit-led lifestyle. *"For it is God who works in you to will and to act in order to fulfill His good purpose." Philippians 2:13*

Q5. Do you desire to have an intimate relationship with God that is Spirit-filled?

FAITHFUL SUBMISSION TO JESUS

God asks us to put Him first in our lives, and when we do, we get clarity about our goals, experience forgiveness for ourselves and others, and walk in God's perfect will. You will learn to commit your life to Jesus and experience daily victories that will lead you to Be Set Free. "For the LORD your God is the one who goes with you to fight for you against your enemies to give you victory." Deuteronomy 20:4

Q6. What are some victories you want to see in your life?

SPEAKING LIFE-GIVING WORDS

By learning to speak words of life that align with God's Word, you will begin to influence your surroundings and relationships by destroying the power of the enemy's words of destruction in your life. *"Do nothing out of selfish ambition or vain conceit, but in humility consider others better than yourselves."* *Philippians 2:3*

Q7. Do you want to be an influence of good for God's Glory and advance His kingdom?

DEVELOPING INTO A VESSEL GOD CAN USE

God has a specific plan and purpose for our lives, but our adversary the devil is attempting to stop this plan and purpose. As you allow God to use your life for His glory, you will learn how to stand in Jesus' authority to overcome sin and the enemy's schemes through your one-on-one time with your Coach. "You have already won a victory over those people, because the Spirit who lives in you is greater than the spirit who lives in the world." 1 John 4:4

Q8. Do you want to learn how to have authority to overcome sin and the enemy's schemes?

MAINTAINING A LIFE OF WORSHIP

Studies have shown everyone, without knowing it, worships something in their lives. We get into bad habits and other problems because we are worshiping something that makes us feel good. Keys to Being Set Free will help guide you to direct your everyday worship to God while learning how it can affect the core of everything you do.

> "I can safely say, on the authority of all that is revealed in the Word of God, that any man or woman on this earth who is bored and turned off by worship is not ready for heaven."– A.W. Tozer

It will take hard work and discipline to be set free, as well as your desire to unlearn old bad habits and replace them with new Godly habits. It is doable, but you must have a never-say-die attitude and persevere no matter what. You can overcome your life hangups and live a transformed life, but it will require your effort to position yourself in God's presence so that you can be known by Jesus. Knowing about Jesus and believing in Jesus is one thing; knowing Jesus intimately and being known by Jesus is quite another.

FAT (FAITHFUL, AVAILABLE, AND TEACHABLE)

Finally, if you possess the qualities of being Faithful, Available, and Teachable (FAT), it is imperative that you fully dedicate yourself to this journey. This entails making necessary adjustments in your life to prioritize it. Actively engage in the process by diligently working through each section of the curriculum.

If you commit to a specific time and day with your coach, ensure that you prioritize it by adapting your schedule accordingly. Regardless of where you currently stand in your Spiritual Journey, it is crucial for all of us to approach it with humility and a broken and contrite spirit. It is impossible to be receptive to learning if you are filled with pride. Therefore, it is important that you set this as a high standard for your own life, as well as for the lives of those whom you will disciple in the future.

It is very important that you pray for God to bring someone into your life while you are going through this curriculum "Keys to Being Set Free" to be your next disciple. We strongly recommend this if you are truly committed to finding freedom. God not only desires for us to grow in our relationship with Him but also to share what we have learned with others. To be obsessed with multiplication is a key ingredient to being set free. God will use you despite your flaws, don't allow Satan to tell you otherwise. Allow the Holy Spirit and the course curriculum to guide you and your time with your disciple every step of the way.

You will be required to start discipling someone during the time you are going through each Key with your coach. Expect this journey together to last 14 to 16 weeks, please set aside at least 1 to 1.5 hours to complete each "KEY". We recommend having weekly or biweekly meetings. We also suggest you read the Key you will be covering with your coach the week before so you are prepared with answers at your meeting.

Q9. Based on what you have read so far, is "Keys to Being Set Free" right for you?

Q10. If so, what do you hope will have occurred in your life by the conclusion of this study?

Q11. Will you be dedicated to completing the curriculum with your Coach and guiding one of your disciples who needs a breakthrough as well?

If you are ready to start your journey through "Keys to Being Set Free" and disciple someone else as God leads, agree to the covenant below and contact your Coach and start with Key 1 right away.

KEYS TO BEING SET FREE COMMITMENT

We (Coach)_____ and (Student)_____ commit to meeting on a weekly or biweekly basis to build a relationship that creates an atmosphere of community and openness for spiritual growth and understanding of God's word.

FOR THIS TO BECOME A REALITY WE COMMIT TO THESE SIMPLE STEPS OF ACCOUNTABILITY.

- We are committed to being on time and at every meeting unless an emergency happens.
- We are willing to be (FAT) Faithful, Available and Teachable
- We will transfer what has been learned to another FAT person in a new Discipleship relationship.

-----------------------------------   ---------------------------------------
Coach Sign   Date

-----------------------------------   ---------------------------------------
Student Sign   Date

KEY 1: THE BEGINNING

Always start and end each "KEY" with PRAYER. Humble yourself before the Lord and allow the Holy Spirit to work through you during your time together. Keep in mind that both the student and the coach should answer each question. Answer the questions honestly with a level of vulnerability. Expect this journey together to last 14 to 16 weeks, please set aside at least 1 to 1.5 hours to complete each "KEY". We recommend meeting weekly or biweekly. We also suggest you read the Key you will be covering with your coach the week before so you are prepared with answers at your meeting.

Keep the discussion to one on one or at most one on two, this is not a group curriculum. Always remember this is a conversation, not a presentation. Let the Holy Spirit move in the conversation, do not rush to get the "Key" done. If you need to pick up where you left off, that is fine, mark your place, and pick back up the following week, but never force or rush the conversation.

(Coach Read)

To "Be Set Free" we must know the truth. *"But when He, the Spirit of truth, comes, He will guide you into all the truth. He will not speak on his own; He will speak only what He hears, and He will tell you what is yet to come." (John 16:13)*

We're so happy that you have chosen to journey through Natural Discipleship's "Keys to Being Set Free". After completing this curriculum, it's possible that your life will never be the same again. Being set free will challenge you to take a step toward the truth about God, about faith, and yourself, regardless of where you are in your journey of faith. Christ redeemed us and made us free for the sake of freedom.

This is what Paul stated in Galatians 5:1, and Jesus Himself said, "that He came to the earth so that we may have life and have it to the full" and in some translations, "more abundantly". (John 10:10) Imagine for a moment that you have an abundance of life. Not merely holding on for dear life, but actively engaging in life without heartache and regret. This passage is saying your life will be brimming with excitement, hope, purpose, and a sense of direction. The kind of life that God has always planned for you to have, is one that looks like this.

WHAT IS AN ABUNDANT LIFE?

An abundant life is not based on material wealth, such as lavish homes, expensive cars, international travel, and more money than we know what to do with. According to the Bible, wealth, prestige, position, and power in this world are not God's priorities for us (1 Corinthians 1:26-29). Clearly, an abundant life does not consist of an abundance of material things; if that were the case, Jesus would have been the richest man alive. Actually, quite the opposite is true, Matthew 8:20 states that *"Foxes have dens and birds have nests, but the Son of Man has no place to lay his head."*

The abundant life that Jesus is referring to is one that is free of worrying about how much money you have, or anything else the world system can offer you. An abundant life is a life that is clean on the inside as well as the outside. Your demeanor is filled with God's love, it is gentle and kind, and you live in complete freedom, knowing that God is in complete control of everything. Joy has taken the place of worry, and patience has taken the place of stress; your world has been turned upside down and now has order, discipline, and purpose.

It is a way of life in which you do not allow the world system to control you, so your mood does not fluctuate as a result of your successes or failures. Jesus instructs us not to be concerned about what we will eat or wear (Matthew 6:25-32), because an abundant life allows us to be content with our choices regardless of our circumstances.

Q1: What is the concept of an "Abundant Life" according to the passage?

Q1A. And how does it differ from worldly perceptions of abundance?

(Student Read)

Today marks the beginning of your journey toward Being Set Free.

Jesus, God's son, came to earth to close the gap between heaven and earth so that people like us may have a relationship with God. God desires to have a personal relationship with you. The path may not be straightforward, but the destination will be worth the effort. During the course of your journey, it will be up to you to determine the lengths to which you are willing to go in order to achieve the abundant life God has promised you.

> You must be willing to unlearn the bad habits that have caused you to place your trust in the world system rather than God's perfect will for you. Jeremiah 29:13 promises us that if we look for Him with all of our hearts, we will discover him. And if we do this, then we will be set free from the pain this world offers us.

Recognizing our inability to overcome our hang-ups on our own is the first step towards freedom, even if you're still trying to figure out what those hang-ups are. A hang-up, as mentioned before, is any and all bad habit(s) or thing(s) we do that are not in accordance with God's perfect will. We develop these hang-ups while attempting to soothe our life's pains and try to make sense of our purpose and identity. We all have them, and we will never be free of them until we learn how to surrender our lives completely to God when circumstances hit us. Our journey through the "Keys to Being Set Free" curriculum will teach us how to apply God's truth while discovering the root causes of our initial wounds that have led to our hang-ups and addictions.

Q2. What is the first step towards freedom according to this passage?

Q2A. And how does this relate to understanding and overcoming our "hang-ups"?

(Coach Read)

In order to accomplish this, we must go all the way back to the Bible's first book, Genesis. There, we will learn about Adam and Eve's decision to go against God's perfect will. By understanding what Adam and Eve did, then we can better understand why we have made poor decisions in our own lives. If we are making decisions that are not in our best interests, we cannot live a life of abundance. So, let's look into why we are tempted to make poor choices or decisions and how it deprives us of God's abundant life for us.

Let's read:

"Then the Lord God planted a garden in Eden in the east, and there he placed the man he had made. The Lord God made all sorts of trees grow up from the ground—trees that were beautiful and that produced delicious fruit. In the middle of the garden, he placed the "Tree of Life" and the "Tree of the Knowledge of Good and Evil". (Genesis 2:8-9) NLT

"But the Lord God warned him, "You may freely eat the fruit of every tree in the garden—except the "Tree of the Knowledge of Good and Evil". If you eat its fruit, you are sure to die." (Genesis 2:16-17) NLT

Adam and Eve were offered the chance to spend all of eternity with God there in the garden, free from stress and fear if they ate from the "Tree of Life". He was their God, and He met all of their needs and requirements for happiness. But there was a "Tree of Knowledge of Good and Evil" in the middle of Eden's Garden. Adam and Eve rejected this freedom and chose to experience the reverse of God's goodness thanks to the tempter and that tree. God gave them the option to choose to obey His instructions because He loved them so much. He desired a genuine relationship with them; He did not want them to be robots who only loved Him because He forced them to.

Q3. What led Adam and Eve to go against God's perfect will in the book of Genesis?

Q4. How does this affect our ability to live a life of abundance as offered by God?

GOD HAS GIVEN EACH OF US A CHOICE

(Student Read)

When we choose the "Tree of Life" living, we are declaring that we wholly trust God with our lives. We are expressing to God that we trust that He will always look after us and that we will never have to worry about anything. By choosing the "Tree of Life", we are basically returning to the Garden of Eden, and the only way into the Garden is through the blood of Jesus. When we choose the "Tree of Knowledge of Good and Evil", we are declaring that we do not want God to be in charge of our lives. We want to work everything out on our own; what God thinks does not matter to us, and we prefer to live our lives as we see fit.

Satan tempted them because of their decision to want to learn more and have more experiences. By telling them there is more to life, he deceived them. They were being told by God that they didn't need anything else. Their lives were written and completed by Him, and everything is finished in Him and it was good.

"You search the Scriptures because you think they give you eternal life. But the Scriptures point to me! Yet you refuse to come to me to receive this life." (John 5:39-40) NLT

According to the "Tree of Knowledge of Good and Evil," a prosperous life is found in material wealth and all that you can achieve through hard work and discipline. It tells you that all you need to do to be happy is live a good life and do enough of the right things, and God will be pleased with your efforts. The reality is that you fail in life, and not just occasionally; you fail frequently, and the cycle of life keeps you starting over again from the beginning. You pick yourself up and continue to try to live your best life through your own efforts, believing in your heart that if you just do good, God will be pleased with you and you can finally get ahead.

Q5. What is the primary difference between choosing the "Tree of Life" and the "Tree of Knowledge of Good and Evil"?

(Coach Read)

Living your life for yourself will never bring you the happiness you seek, it will only bring you chaos and false intimacy. The "Tree of Knowledge of Good and Evil" is a deception that we buy into without even knowing that we are living according to its standards. However, the "Tree of Life" declares that if you live your life trusting Jesus, He will always take care of you, and accept and love you just as you are. True freedom comes when we learn to choose Jesus over choosing ourselves and our desires.

"And since we have been made right in God's sight by the blood of Christ, He will certainly save us from God's condemnation". (Romans 5:9) NLT. The "Tree of Knowledge of Good and Evil" teaches that you must obey God to make Him happy with you, but the "Tree of Life" teaches that you should obey God out of your delight in Him. *"For it is the goodness of God that leads us to repentance." (Romans 2:4)*

Q6. Why would living your life for yourself never bring you the happiness you seek?

RELIGION IS DISGUISED AS THE "TREE OF LIFE" BUT IT'S ACTUALLY THE "TREE OF KNOWLEDGE OF GOOD AND EVIL"

(Student Read)

Religion is a collection of rules based on the "Tree of Knowledge of Good and Evil," as we like to say, Religion Sucks. It only places demands on individuals that no one can ever meet. Religion does not seek to elevate others above themselves; rather, it seeks to govern people's feelings about themselves. The "Tree of Life" is a loving connection with God founded on the assurance that he will never abandon you or forsake you. It always searches for ways to forgive and encourage one another, and it never puts others down. It is patient, kind, and does not maintain a record of wrongs; it does not envy or boast about accomplishments.

Q7. What is the difference between religion and relationship with God?

(Coach Read)

We start feeling guilt and shame when we partake from the "Tree of Knowledge of Good and Evil". We possess a spiritual awareness that we have committed wrongdoing and we try to find ways to alleviate our negative emotions. At times, we attempt to earn validation from others, whether it be a spouse, boss, parent, or peer. We yearn for their approval so intensely that we exhaust ourselves or compromise our health and morality.

As the acceptance of others becomes the foremost measure in our lives, we sacrifice our own beliefs, convictions, and standards in order to fit in. Another tactic that Satan employs is making us look like the Pharisees. We turn to religion as a means to cope with our past mistakes. Without fully surrendering ourselves to God and freeing ourselves from our previous sins, we pursue avenues, such as religion, to find peace.

> **People who engage in religious activities constantly strive to make an impression on others within the religious community. They appear righteous on the surface, but, similar to the Pharisees in the Bible, they have never fully surrendered their lives to God.**

Consequently, they harbor lies, deceit, and darkness within them. Similarly, these individuals are quick to judge others and hold themselves in high regard. They often mention how hard they have worked to restore their life and look down on those who used to be in the position they were in. They now perceive themselves as an important individual, so they engage in actions that seek attention.

However, they are unwilling to let people scrutinize their lives due to the numerous lies they have to hide and become defensive. These types of individuals are prone to react with anger if they are confronted or questioned about something that seems amiss. They convince themselves that they are helping people, yet in reality, they are just broken individuals who end up hurting others. Eventually, like the Pharisees their falsehoods and reprehensible behavior will be exposed, resulting in negative consequences that adversely impact the lives of many.

Q8. What similarities are drawn between individuals who use religion to cope with their past mistakes, and the Pharisees mentioned in the Bible?

(Student Read)

There are many individuals in the Church today who have unresolved issues from their past and are struggling with hang-ups and addictions. These individuals have failed to address their own sins and instead tried to hide them by seeking validation from others. As a consequence, numerous individuals within the Church present themselves as genuine believers but, in reality, are deceitful and harmful, just like the wolves disguised as sheep described in (Matthew 7:15). Their actions have caused significant harm to people's lives, leading many to leave the Church and lose trust in anyone associated with it.

Shockingly, these individuals who claim to follow Christ have caused irreparable damage and made decisions on behalf of others. They assert that they have a deeper understanding of God and that God speaks through them, demanding that everyone listen to them. However, most of the time, their motives are self-centered, and their decisions are based on personal opinions and emotions rather than on the Holy Spirit.

Rarely do they genuinely convey God's truth in a comprehensible manner, without hidden motives. It's important to note that these individuals are not just regular churchgoers; They can also include Pastors, leaders, and others who have experienced past pain and have not properly dealt with their own suffering. This is what religion can do to people who base their worth on their performance and not on what Jesus did for them on the cross.

Q9. What are the detrimental effects caused by individuals within the Church who have unresolved personal issues?

Q9A. And how do they base their worth on their performance rather than on the sacrifice of Jesus?

WE WORK HARD TO PLEASE GOD

(Coach Read)

Sometimes, we attempt to impress God by attempting to prove ourselves to Him. We strive to earn His approval and please Him with our good works. You might say, "Look God, I have been so devoted to you." Or, "I am involved in so much ministry, surely God is pleased with me." We become satisfied with demonstrating our worth to God.

We work hard to meet the standards of being good enough, mission-focused enough, and spiritually capable enough. We may even secretly hold the belief that, despite being forgiven through Christ, God's favor is dependent on our performance after salvation. We convince ourselves that if we engage in enough spiritual practices, we will achieve the spiritual closeness we desire.

We believe that we can repay God or that our good deeds make us more favorable in His eyes compared to other Christians who are less worthy. It is commendable to have God as our moral guide, but the issue arises when we fail to acknowledge that His love for us is complete and unwavering, regardless of our accomplishments and our imperfections. It is never about what we can do for God; it always revolves around what God has already done for us.

> Satan deceives us with the notion that we can attain God's presence by being good enough. This falsehood persists because we can never be good enough; we all fall short of God's glory. The only way we can enter heaven is because God loved us first and sent His Son, Jesus, to die for us. Do not believe that you can earn your way to God or gain special privileges with Him. Instead, get to know Jesus personally, learn to love Him with your whole heart and accept God's truth for your life.

Religion is our effort (Tree of Knowledge of Good and Evil), Relationship with Jesus is His effort (Tree of Life), we simply bask in His glory and live in the Freedom He offers us. The only thing God desires from us is our worship and fellowship with Himself, not our efforts to please Him to earn God's favor.

Q10. What misconceptions might Christians have about earning God's favor and approval?

Q11. How does this misunderstanding impact their spiritual journey and understanding of God's love?

OUR RESPONSE DETERMINES OUR VICTORY

(Student Read)

The first step we must take to triumph over living in the "Tree of Knowledge of Good and Evil" is that we must be convinced that we are in desperate need of God in every aspect of our lives. That begins with a daily prayer life and a consistent effort to meditate on God's word. Getting to know and love Jesus is a daily process, just like any other relationship. Take the time to read His words and then obey His commands.

I recall God speaking to me in my home garage after many years of living in the "Tree of Knowledge of Good and Evil". He said, "Son, I love you, and I ask again, are you ready to do things my way?" Keep in mind that I was crying and on my knees in excruciating pain as a result of my life choices. That's when I told God, "Yes, I'm ready to do things your way."

The first piece of advice He gave me was to get to know Him intimately. I quickly realized that spending daily quiet time with Jesus was the most important thing I needed to do to get myself out of the hole I had dug for myself.

Q12. What has been your experience with spending quality quiet time with God daily?

\--

\--

Q13. What is the first step one must take to overcome living in the "Tree of Knowledge of Good and Evil"?

\--

\--

(Coach Read)

"If you love me, obey my commandments." (John 14:15) NLT. You are encouraged to doubt God's love for you by the "Tree of Knowledge of Good and Evil". You are reminded by the "Tree of Life" of how tremendous God's love for you is simply by the fact that He gave His life as a sacrifice for you. For the first time in my life, I felt utter shame in my garage and realized that I am not a very good person, as I thought I was.

God opened my eyes with His loving grace so that I can see myself in His Holy presence. It was there that I felt undone, just like Isaiah did in Isaiah 6, I couldn't speak, all I felt was that I was dirty and I needed to be cleaned.

Up until that point, I had always wondered if God truly loved me, and I had blamed Him for everything. But it was in that dark moment that God said, "I love you, Son." He never once pointed out my flaws; he simply loved me with a love I can't adequately describe here. Satan wants us to believe that living in the "Tree of Knowledge of Good and Evil" means you can't experience God's love, but I can assure you that you can, and it's found in the "Tree of Life", and His love will surpass all of your comprehension.

Q14. How does the "Tree of Life" relate to a person's understanding of God's love?

Q15. Have you ever wondered whether God truly loves you? Share your story.

(Student Read)

According to a set of laws, religion expects you to serve God by following them completely. These regulations are impossible to follow and will ultimately result in your life being condemned. These laws were repealed by Jesus' death, burial, and resurrection, freeing us from the shackles of sin. *"Don't misunderstand why I have come. I did not come to abolish the law of Moses or the writings of the prophets. No, I came to accomplish their purpose."* *(Matthew 5:17)*

We start to interact with the living God when we fall in love with Jesus. Our everyday interactions are based on Jesus' love for us, not on our efforts to win His favor, that is Religion. My garage experience taught me that I did not have a deep personal relationship with God. I knew a lot about Him, and knew his story, but I didn't know Him the way He wanted me to.

I chose to accept His free gift of Grace rather than try to work my way to heaven through religion. I realized there was nothing I could do to please Him and that His Son had already done everything I needed for me.

Q16. What realization did the author have about their relationship with God?

Q16A. And how did it impact their approach towards religion and grace?

Q17.Have you ever served God through rules based on organized religion? Share your story.

(Coach Read)

Do not buy into Satan's deception that you must perform certain actions to earn God's acceptance. Respond to these falsehoods with God's truth, and speak life into your thinking.

> *"For God did not send His Son into the world to condemn the world, but in order that the world might be saved through him". (John 3:17) "So now there is no condemnation for those who belong to Christ Jesus". (Romans 8:1)*

The "Tree of Knowledge of Good and Evil" will always result in you thinking that you are not good enough. Jesus claims He will never condemn you, but apart from Him, you are already condemned. Condemnation brings guilt and shame and ultimately pushes you away from God. But when you choose to accept that God never condemns you, you now begin to live in the freedom that is found only in the "Tree of Life".

So, when we commit sins in the future, with the help of the Holy Spirit, the lifestyle of living in accordance with God's will, referred to as the "Tree of Life", will make us aware of our sins and show us that the things we are engaging in are not beneficial for our well-being. This process will always be conducted with genuine love and is intended for our ultimate good. It's important to note that sinning does not mean we lose favor with God; Rather, He wants us to rely on Him and trust Him completely with our lives. He will constantly remind us of His great love for us and assure us that nothing can come between us and His love.

"What shall we say about such wonderful things as these? If God is for us, who can ever be against us? Since he did not spare even his own Son but gave him up for us all, won't he also give us everything else? Who dares accuse us whom God has chosen for his own? No one—for God himself has given us right standing with himself.

Who then will condemn us? No one—for Jesus died for us and was raised to life for us, and he is sitting in the place of honor at God's right hand, pleading for us". I am convinced that nothing can ever separate us from God's love. Neither death nor life, neither angels nor demons, * neither our fears for today nor our worries about tomorrow—not even the powers of hell can separate us from God's love. No power in the sky above or in the earth below—indeed, nothing in all creation will ever be able to separate us from the love of God that is revealed in Christ Jesus our Lord." (Romans 8:31-39)

Q18. How does the belief that God never condemns us, regardless of our sins, lead to a new lifestyle of living in accordance with God's will?

Q19. What if we have trouble or calamity, or are persecuted, hungry, destitute, or in danger, or threatened with death in our lives, does it mean Jesus no longer loves us? Share your thoughts.

Q20. How could you speak life to yourself next time Satan wants to condemn you for your actions?

(Student Read)

Always guard your Heart from choosing to go back to your old life. "Today I have given you the choice between life and death, between blessings and curses. Now I call on heaven and earth to witness the choice you make. Oh, that you would choose life so that you and your descendants might live!" (Deuteronomy 30:19) NLT

The "Tree of Knowledge of Good and Evil" will try to convince you that your previous life was superior, but was it, really?

The "Tree of Life" will remind us that it is important to make sacrifices in order to build a relationship with Jesus, as eternal peace is valuable. We need to remain steadfast in our faith if we want to protect our hearts. By doing so, we can resist the devil and follow the command to submit ourselves to God (James 4:7). It is also crucial that we pay attention to God's word, as stated in (Proverbs 4:20-23) "My child, listen carefully to my words and pay attention to what I say."

The decision of the "Tree of Knowledge of Good and Evil" will always lead you to despair, whereas the choice of the "Tree of Life" would always result in joy, peace and happiness.

Q21. What are some ways you can guard your heart from going back to your old life?

> **Pray: Pray that God will continue to show you that this life is not about you but about Him and His love for you. Confess any areas in your life where you might have been trying to please others or God.**

KEY 2 WHY OUR CULTURE INFLUENCES US

(Coach Read)

People differ in terms of their values, beliefs, and perspectives. Cultural differences can influence how people make decisions. It's vital to understand how these distinctions affect how you interpret and approach the decision-making process when deciding which decision is best.

Who you are, where you live, and your values all influence how you make decisions. We might easily become confused or distracted from a culture that is taking us down a path of ruin if our values are not aligned with what God's word says.

The world culture is filled with evil and darkness, and the only way to counteract the effects of our civilization is to live in the "Tree of Life."

The "Tree of Life" is more than just the setting for a biblical story; it is a way of life. To discover how, we must delve deeper into Genesis 1, the first biblical text that details the creation of the universe. God is described as the Creator and Ruler who possesses absolute authority and dominion over everything. Adam and Eve, their transgression, and the two trees in the garden are also discussed.

If we wish to be set free from the burdens of this world, we must comprehend both of these narratives, everything we learn in the Bible hinges on it.

Every day we have a choice of living in the promises of the "Tree of Life or in the lies of the "Tree of Knowledge of Good and Evil". The "Tree of Life" will bring you freedom, grace, eternal life, forgiveness, and the knowledge that God is good. The "Tree of Knowledge of Good and Evil", will bring you bondage, religion or law, eternal death and make you believe that God is judging and condemning you.

When studying the Bible, it is often wise to locate the first mention of a topic. In our journey together, we will learn to walk toward Being Set Free while in communion with God. We will discover how our culture is what divides us from God and why we prefer bondage over freedom or liberty.

Q1. What does the "Tree of Life" represent according to the context of the passage?

Q1A. And how is it different from the "Tree of Knowledge of Good and Evil"?

(Student Read)

The Bible reveals to us in Genesis 3 that this is the point in time when humanity first became estranged from God. Before Adam and Eve made their decision to eat from the tree that held the "Knowledge of both Good and Evil," they had a harmonious relationship with God. Adam was given dominion and power over everything that God had created.

If they did not have this connection, Adam would never be in a position of authority. Because Adam and Eve disobeyed God by eating the forbidden fruit, they lost their authority.

Through trickery and open disobedience, the serpent was able to seize the authority and control that God had given man. According to the Bible, Satan's goal was to raise his throne to a position of prominence that would rival that of God's dominion, (Isaiah 14:13). Man lacked the authority and influence necessary to establish rulership prior to his fall from grace. The culture for man has shifted and now Satan has authority over man. In (John 12:31), Jesus identified Satan as the one who rules over this world.

Q2. What event in Genesis 3 led to humanity's estrangement from God, resulting in a shift of authority from man to Satan?

(Coach Read)

According to Colossians 1:21), it states that in the past, we were distant from God. We were His adversaries, and the wicked thoughts and actions we had kept us away from Him. Sin causes division, and because of this division, we lose both our freedom and the authority over Satan that God gives to His children.

However, through the death and resurrection of Jesus Christ, this separation came to an end. Through the resurrection, He restored our relationship with God. As mentioned in Colossians 1:20), God used the shedding of Christ's blood on the cross to reconcile everything in heaven and on earth.

Before Adam and Eve ate from the fruit of the "Tree of Knowledge of Good and Evil", their way of life was based on peace and fellowship with God. After they ate the tree's fruit, their way of life shifted towards a sinful lifestyle controlled by Satan.

> You cannot experience true freedom from the culture around us if you refuse to acknowledge that without Jesus' shed blood, you are cut off from God, you lack all power, and have no other means to interact with Him. Jesus told His disciples that *"He Is the way, the truth, and the life. No one can come to the Father except through Him". (John 14:6) NLT*

Make sure you are resolved in your decision to accept Jesus as your personal Savior before we continue. Or if you previously committed your life to Jesus and now feel the need to change your ways, this is the perfect opportunity to do so. Repent of your sins and align your heart, because this is the first step toward a life of freedom from the culture that has dictated your life for many years.

Q3. What is the role of Jesus Christ's death and resurrection, in restoring our relationship with God?

Q.4 What does the passage imply about the role of accepting Jesus as a personal savior in achieving freedom from the influence of our culture?

A CLOSER EXAMINATION OF THE ORIGINAL SIN THAT CAUSED DIVISION

(Student Read)

The Lord God made all sorts of trees grow up from the ground—trees that were beautiful and that produced delicious fruit. In the middle of the garden, he placed the "Tree of Life" and the "Tree of the Knowledge of Good and Evil." (Genesis 2:9)

But the Lord God warned him, *"You may freely eat the fruit of every tree in the garden— except the "Tree of the Knowledge of Good and Evil." If you eat its fruit, you are sure to die."* (Genesis 2:16-17)

(Read Genesis 3:1-8 out loud together)

After eating from the fruit of the "Tree of the Knowledge of Good and Evil", Adam and Eve felt ashamed. They hid from God and covered themselves out of humiliation. *Genesis 3:9 says "Then the Lord God called to the man, "Where are you?"*

Q5. Given that He is God and should be aware of their location, why did God call Adam and Eve in this manner?

(Coach Read)

> **Warning:** You don't want to miss this part: Adam and Eve hid, and God went seeking after them. According to the Bible, **God is looking for wicked sinful people to save.** The fact that God loves sinful man is evidenced by the fact that He sent his Son, Jesus, to save people.

Consider if you had a 16-year-old son who was caught stealing money from his workplace. Instead of contacting the cops, the store owner showed your son kindness and brought him to you. When your son enters your home, he instantly drops his head in shame, and when he looks up, he notices that you are angry. Your first reaction is to tell him how wrong he was and to ask him what he was thinking. Your first instinct is to discipline your son so that he never does something like that again.

But this is not how God reacted when Adam and Eve were caught in their sin. God never condemns us or attempts to make us feel guilty or ashamed; our sin does that. God pursued Adam and Eve in love in order to reestablish a relationship with them.

Granted, sin separated them from God, but it never altered God's love for them or desire to fellowship with them. What if your son came in and was not repentant, claiming, "I didn't do anything wrong?" I was only borrowing the money; I planned to repay it. How would your relationship with your son be if he showed no remorse? Would you stop loving him? Of course not, but your relationship with him would not be as close as it should be. It would be difficult to have an intimate relationship with your son in the way that it is intended when he refuses to repent of his wrongdoing.

> **Sin separates us from God; only repentance allows us to have close fellowship with Him.** He never ceases seeking or loving us; all He wants is for us to establish close communion with Him. We want to discipline our son, yet God sometimes punishes us, especially when we know better (Hebrews 12:6). But, perhaps more importantly, God's approach to us is to love us despite our sins.

Not in a condemning, angry, pointing-the-finger sort of way, *but in a Father forgive them because they know not what they're doing,* type of way *(Luke 23:34)*. What if we loved people the way God loves us? What if we stopped pointing fingers and expressing our anger at them and simply loved them as Jesus taught us with gentleness and agape love?

It is His love coupled with His kindness towards us that leads us to repentance (Romans 2:4), not His condemnation and making us feel awful for our actions (Romans 8:1). James 4:8 says *"Come close to God, and God will come close to you. Wash your hands, you sinners; purify your hearts, for your loyalty is divided between God and the world"*. Before the fall, Adam and Eve's loyalty was solely to God, but after the fall, the world became a distraction between them and God. God is Holy, and to enter His presence, we must repent and draw near to Him.

Q6. What does the Bible say about God's reaction to Adam and Eve's sin?

Q6A. And how does it reflect His love and pursuit for sinful man?

Q7. How could our relationship with God be affected by sin and the lack of repentance?

Q8. What lessons can we learn from His approach to dealing with our sin?

(Student Read)

God will never leave His children behind; we are the ones who decide to leave Him. God is constantly there, looking for us and longing for fellowship with us. By consuming the forbidden fruit, Adam and Eve had acknowledged that they committed sin. When we favor the ways of the world's culture over God's promises, we too are guilty of sin.

The foundation of world culture is enhancing one's self-image into the image of their god. Whatever truth they consider superior becomes their god, and their behavior will reflect their beliefs. When in the story the son sinned, his god became his notion that what he needed at the time was money, and it was worth the risk to him. However, the Bible warns that our sin will find us out (Numbers 32:23), and that no matter how far we run from God in our wrongdoing, we will eventually be caught and face the consequences.

In those moments, we must choose whether to yield to a loving merciful God or to continue running from Him in quest of our next truth based on how we wish to see the world apart from God.

The world operates according to the efforts of its inhabitants and is governed by Satan's falsehoods. Anything that we place our faith in besides the God of the Bible is a deception perpetrated by Satan. Once we have exhausted ourselves and realized that we cannot continue living a life apart from the God of the Bible, we begin to see ourselves in His light and recognize how depraved we truly are.

When we have addictions, hang-ups, or self-protection in our lives, it is because we have made other gods more essential than God. This reality forces us to confront the fact that we have sinned, and we think God will not be pleased with us, so we hide.

God does not respond to His children in wrath but with grace. We don't need to hide behind our hang-ups, addictions and fig leaves any longer. He loves you period and wants you to run to him and stop hiding. As we will learn in the journey of being set free, the lie that God does not love you or desire fellowship with you is false.

No amount of sin can separate you from His love, but the truth is that we are still tempted to flee from Him when we sin. All God wants from us is a restored fellowship, but we've got to stop running and just accept His forgiveness. He is kind and loving and does not condemn you.

Q9. What is the significance of realizing our sinful nature?

Q9A. And why is it important to stop running from God and accept His forgiveness, instead of aligning with worldly culture?

ADDITIONAL FACTS REGARDING THE "FRUIT OF THE TREE OF KNOWLEDGE OF GOOD AND EVIL"

(Coach Read)

The Fruit gives us knowledge of right and wrong.

What exactly was the fruit? Was it an actual apple, or was it something else? Most Bible Scholars are uncertain about the fruit's precise nature, but we know that Adam and Eve were different after they partook of it. After their actions, their minds were open to new concepts, worldviews, and perceptions of good and evil. God, before they ate of the fruit, was essentially telling Adam and Eve that it would change their way of thinking; it would drive a wedge between them.

> It would alter their viewpoint and they will no longer be able to relate to and comprehend Him. But Satan lied to them and said, "Thinking this way won't affect you. As God is saying to you, it will only make things better."

When we pursue quick fixes for our problems, we convince ourselves that what we are doing will only make things better. Most of the time, our goals are not to harm ourselves, but to assist us in coping with what we are experiencing. As Adam and Eve were told, you can't know everything unless you attempt it (take the fruit). The same thing occurs when we convince ourselves that our actions that are contrary to God's truth are acceptable.

It is essential to note that God did not condemn knowledge; He simply stated that He has all knowledge and that you do not need to seek truth elsewhere.

Q10. What does Adam and Eve consuming the fruit illustrate about human behavior and our tendency to seek solutions different from God's truth?

(Student Read)

God desires us to seek knowledge as long as it is based on God's truth. God foretold through the prophet Hosea, that Israel would be annihilated due to their ignorance and lack of knowledge. (Hosea 4:6) God desires that we seek Him first before we try anything else the world has to give. The issue is the motivation behind the action, not necessarily the under-standing. We want answers now, so we seek methods that will assist apart from consulting with God first and His word. Don't believe Satan's lie that we can find knowledge or other truths that are better than God's.

The world system will teach us that we seek knowledge because we want to learn as much as possible about the world around us and the people in it. We use knowledge to make informed decisions and to solve problems. People have been seeking knowledge since the beginning of time. We have been told that early humans learned how to make fire, how to hunt and gather food, and how to build shelters. They also learned how to communicate with each other.

In the Bible, the word "knowledge" refers to an understanding, realization, or acknowledg-ment. To "know" something is to perceive or recognize it. Knowledge is frequently used in Scripture to refer to a greater appreciation for something or a relationship with someone. The Bible makes it plain that knowing God is the most valuable information a person can have. But it is also obvious that simply knowing God exists is insufficient; knowledge of God must include a genuine appreciation for and relationship with Him.

We do not seek knowledge so that we gain an understanding of our needs or wants. We seek knowledge so that we gain a deeper understanding of God. God offers knowledge as a gift from His vast treasury of knowledge. God's creation, according to Psalm 19:2, demonstrates the Creator's understanding: *"Night after night [the skies] display knowledge."*

As Paul reminds us in Romans 1:19-20, the immensity of God's wisdom and creative might are constantly on show and are clearly visible in all He has created. God's knowledge is not just limitless, but absolute: *"Oh, the depth of the riches of God's wisdom and knowledge! How unsearchable his judgments, and his paths beyond tracing out!" (Romans 11:33)*. When

God came to earth as Jesus Christ, He became the personification of knowledge: "Christ, in whom are hidden all the treasures of wisdom and knowledge." (Colossians 2:2-3).

Our pursuit of knowledge should never lead us to make decisions solely based on our discoveries. Instead, we should seek guidance from God, as His knowledge will guide our future actions. Ultimately, everything stems from and concludes with Him. By doing so, we transfer authority to God, and the influence of worldly culture no longer holds power over us, when it comes to seeking knowledge.

Q11. How does the concept of seeking knowledge from a Biblical perspective differ from the worldly system of acquiring knowledge?

Q12. What role should God's wisdom and guidance play in our process of decision-making?

(Coach Read)

Apart from God, human knowledge is flawed. It is also referred to as worthless in the Bible since it is not tempered by love. (1 Corinthians 13:2). Man's knowledge tends to make him feel proud. "Knowledge expands, but love expands." (1 Corinthians 8:1). As a result, seeking knowledge for its own sake without seeking God is foolishness. *"Then I applied myself to the comprehension of wisdom... but I discovered that this, too, is chasing after the wind." For with great learning comes great anguish; the more the knowledge, the greater the grief." (Ecclesiastes 1:17-18).*

Worldly knowledge is false information that is completely opposed to the truth, and Paul exhorts us to *"turn away from godless chatter and the opposing ideas of what is falsely called knowledge, which some have professed and thus have wandered from the faith." (1 Timothy 6:20-21).* Human knowledge is opposite to God's understanding and hence is not knowledge at all; rather, it is foolishness.

Knowledge, according to the Christian, implies a relationship. When the Bible states, *"Adam knew Eve his wife" (Genesis 4:1) NKJV,* it suggests he had a bodily relationship with her. This is also how spiritual partnerships are described.

"I am the good shepherd; I know my sheep, and my sheep know me," Jesus said of His redeeming connection with those who follow Him. (John 10:14). "You will know the truth, and the truth will set you free," He also promised His disciples. (John 8:32).

In contrast, Jesus told the unbelievers, *"You do not know [my Father]." (Verse 55).* To know Christ, then, is to believe in Him, to follow Him, to have a relationship with Him, to love and be loved by Him. (See also John 14:7; 1 Corinthians 8:3; Galatians 4:9; and 2 Timothy 2:19.) Growing in God's knowledge is an element of Christian maturity that all Christians should experience as we "grow in the grace and knowledge of our Lord and Savior Jesus Christ." (2 Peter 3:18).

Q13. What do Christians believe about the difference between human knowledge and God's knowledge?

Q14. How is this knowledge linked to personal relationships according to the verses we read here in the Bible?

GODLY WISDOM VERSUS WORLDLY WISDOM

(Student Read)

Since the beginning of time, humans have craved wisdom. God genuinely approves of this desire. In the book of 1 Kings, God appears to King Solomon in a dream and asks him, *"What do you want?" I will give it to you if you ask!* Solomon requested one thing: the knowledge to lead Israel and the capacity to distinguish between good and evil.

> *"The Lord was pleased that Solomon had asked for wisdom. So, God replied, "Because you have asked for wisdom in governing my people with justice and have not asked for a long life or*

> *wealth or the death of your enemies— I will give you what you asked for! I will give you a wise and understanding heart such as no one else has had or ever will have!*
>
> *And I will also give you what you did not ask for—riches and fame! No other king in all the world will be compared to you for the rest of your life!" (1 Kings 3:10-13) NLT*

Godly wisdom comes from God and respects God. Godly wisdom begins with fear of God and leads to a holy living. Worldly wisdom, on the other hand, is preoccupied with pleasing oneself rather than honoring God. With worldly wisdom, we can become educated, street-smart, and have "common sense" that allows us to effectively play the world's game. Godly wisdom allows us to plan for eternity.

We exchange earthly values for biblical values with godly wisdom. (1 John 2:15–16). We realize that we are heirs of another kingdom and make decisions that reflect that choice. (Philippians 1:27; 3:20). Having godly wisdom means striving to see life through God's eyes and acting appropriately.

Q15. What difference does the passage highlight between worldly wisdom and Godly wisdom?

(Coach Read)

The book of Proverbs in the Bible is classified as "wisdom literature". Proverbs is full of life-changing advice. Many proverbs contrast the wise and the foolish and warn against repeating foolish behavior. (e.g., Proverbs 3:35; 14:24; 15:7; 26:11). Everyone makes mistakes, but the wise learn from them and take steps to prevent making them again. The stupid or unwise may repeatedly make the same error and never learn their lesson.

God-given insight is very different from conventional wisdom. Differentiating between the two is possible by looking at their individual traits. First God's wisdom is unadulterated, devoted to peace and harmony, gentle at all times, ready to submit to others, abundant in mercy and good works, without partiality, and always sincere.

Where knowledge from the world is Jealous, self-centered, materialistic, unspiritual, driven by evil desires, with a win-at-all-cost mentality.

We make decisions all the time, and even the simplest ones can be made with God's wisdom. By imitating God, we can grow more like Him by using Godly wisdom. His knowledge draws us nearer to Him. The wisdom of this world causes us to sin, which separates us from God. *James 1:5 says "If you need wisdom, ask our generous God, and he will give it to you. He will not rebuke you for asking."*

Adam and Eve did not accept God's wisdom when they chose to eat of the "Tree of Knowledge of Good and Evil". They rejected it and the fruit ended up bringing death upon them. *(Genesis 2:16-17) NLT says, "The Lord God commanded the man, saying, you may surely eat of every tree of the garden, but of the "Tree of the Knowledge of Good and Evil" you shall not eat, for in the day that you eat of it you will surely die".*

Q16. How do the Book of Proverbs and the story of Adam and Eve showcase the contrast between wisdom from God and wisdom from the world?

(Student Read)

Consuming fruit from the "Tree of Knowledge of Good and Evil" in the pursuit of godliness is lethal. Satan did not tempt Eve with open defiance. *"Go ahead and eat the fruit, he said. It will make you like God."* Satan tempted Eve by appealing to her desire to be like God. It is important to note that the desire to know everything runs counter to the desire to trust God completely. We would rather gain knowledge and try to control our own lives than rely on God to provide for us.

(Genesis 3:22-24 ESV) says *"Behold, the man has become like one of us in knowing good and evil, therefore the Lord God sent him out from the garden of Eden to work the ground from which he was taken"* God is Holy, and He cannot tolerate sin, so he had to expel them.

"It's your sins that have cut you off from God. Because of your sins, he has turned away and will not listen anymore." (Isaiah 59:2) NLT

Adam and Eve did not die physically at that moment, but they did die spiritually. Death entered the human race as a result of Adam's disobedience. Because of this, we are all born spiritually dead in need of a new life. The good news is that we now have access to the "Tree of Life" thanks to Jesus. Over time we will become more like Him, and our culture will start to have less influence on us as we pursue Him in our desire for godly wisdom.

Q17. When do we need God's wisdom?

Q17A. What steps do we need to take to apply His wisdom to our daily life?

(Coach Read)

Sin does not begin with the act itself, but rather with our thoughts. We must be extremely cautious about what we allow into our minds. There are sinful fruit temptations in every aspect of our lives today. For instance, in the TV shows and movies we watch, in our music, and on the internet, if you're not careful, all of these could cause you problems for the rest of your life.

Similarly, reading and studying certain ideologies has the potential to pollute your mind and lead you to be separated from God's perfect will.

> *"The woman was convinced. She saw that the tree was beautiful and its fruit looked delicious, and she wanted the wisdom it would give her. So, she took some of the fruit and ate it. Then she gave some to her husband, who was with her, and he ate it, too." (Genesis 3:6) NLT.* Even though what you're seeing looks good, if God says it's not good, we should run away from it as fast as we can.

Like Eve, it's easy for us to fall into Satan's trap and make a choice that can change our lives in a big way. But even worse, the choices we make can drag other people down with us, and we can be held accountable for more than just our own decisions.

"Therefore, concentrate your minds, with the strictest self-control, and fix your hopes on the blessing that is coming for you at the appearing of Jesus Christ" (1 Peter 1:13) OEB. Don't let the society around you convince you to think things are great when they are actually pushing us farther away from God.

We have to tell ourselves that God's ways are the best and that Satan's and the world's ways are not best for us, but a lie. In fact, when you're tempted to follow the world system, you should say out loud, **"No, that's a lie from Satan," and then say, "In the name of Jesus, get out of my mind."** Then quote God's word into your life.

Q18. How can we protect our minds from allowing Satan to get us to believe the world's standards over God's?

(Student Read)

God never turned His back on Adam and Eve, it was Adam and Eve's eyes that were open to see God's Holiness. That is why they hid themselves from God and covered up their nakedness. They were ashamed and afraid of God's reaction to their choice. *"When the cool evening breezes were blowing, the man and his wife heard the Lord God walking about in the garden. So, they hid from the Lord God among the trees (Genesis 3:8) NLT"* Adam and Eve believed Satan's lie that God would punish them, but the truth is that God sought them out despite their sin.

> *(1 John 4:8) says "God is love"* and in *(1 Peter 4:8) says "God's love covers a multitude of sins."* When we see God's heart for us, we will learn to run to Him instead of away from Him. **From the very beginning, God has pursued us and continues to do so.** After Adam and Eve sinned, they did not run toward God; they ran away from Him, hiding among the trees of the garden.

Jesus used the parables of the lost sheep and the lost coin (Luke 15:3–10) to teach us that God pursues us. Jesus wanted us to understand the heart of God and that He knows each person intimately (Matthew 10:29–31; Psalm 139:13).

God's passionate love for us was demonstrated when He sent His beloved Son to die in our place (John 3:16–18; 2 Corinthians 5:21; 9:15).

He reached down to us because we couldn't reach Him through our efforts. He pursues us even when we are stubborn: *"I revealed myself to those who did not ask for me; I was found by those who did not seek me,"* God said to the Israelites. *'Here I am, here I am,' I said to a nation that did not call my name. I've been holding out my hands all day to an obstinate people who walk in bad ways, pursuing their own imaginations—a people who constantly provoke me to my face" (Isaiah 65:1–3).*

> **If we do not protect our hearts from being influenced by the culture around us, we may be misled by Satan's deceptive words and ultimately make decisions that go against God's teachings and His intention for our well-being.**

Q19. How does the Bible illustrate God's relentless pursuit of us even when we stray?

Q20. How does understanding God's love this way help us become free from our cultural influences?

> Pray: Ask God to help you identify areas in your life where the world has control over you. Ask him to show you what changes you need to make to put Him first. Praise Him for accepting you exactly as you are and for pursuing you despite your flaws.

KEY 3 OVERCOMING VICTIMIZATION, SHAME, AND REGRET

(Coach Read)

The dictionary says the meaning of victimization is "hostility and ill-treatment, especially because of one's background or beliefs. The act or process of singling someone out for cruel or unfair treatment, typically through physical or emotional abuse. It could be an unwanted sexual advance. It is an action or fact of victimizing someone for personal gain and or punishment."

The "Tree of Knowledge of Good and Evil" will always be the source of victimization and shame. Its goal is to abuse or rob a person of their innocence and joy. When we are victimized or are the victimizers, we are controlling the moment that allows evil to reign.

Abuse is a simple term that can encompass a wide range of actions. This is due to the fact that there are individuals who succumb to evil and our world is filled with imperfections, which means that everyone will experience some form of abuse or victimization at some point in their lives (as referenced in Genesis 3 and Romans 5:12).

We may face mental abuse from a spouse, a demanding boss, a trusted friend, or emotional abuse from a defiant child, or spiritual abuse from someone in the Church who is legalistic. It is important to realize that anyone, at any given time, can either fall victim to abuse or become the perpetrator themselves.

A victim is someone who did not choose to be hurt by what is happening to him or her. If the victim had a choice, they would not let their humanity be used in this way.

Q1. How does the "Tree of Knowledge of Good and Evil" relate to the concept of abuse and victimization in various areas of one's life?

(Student Read)

Abusing others as a victim goes against God's nature, which is good, compassionate, and kind. The realization is that, hurt people, hurt other people. Jesus taught that those who harm and lead others into sin will face His anger (Luke 17:2). If you have been victimized by someone, Jesus assures us that we can turn to Him for help and He will heal our pain (Psalm 34:18). He does not judge us for the wrongs done to us. Jesus Himself endured terrible abuse, so He understands how to comfort us in our suffering (Isaiah 52:14; Hebrews 4:15; John 15:13). He is always interceding for His children, particularly those who are hurting. When we reach out to Him, He extends His grace to us (Romans 8:34).

No matter how deep our wounds may be, God has the power to mend our brokenness, restore us, and make things right once again. He promises that if we come to Him through His Son, Jesus Christ, He will take off our dirty clothes and dress us in His perfect righteousness. (Isaiah 64:6; 1 Corinthians 5:21).

Q2. How does Jesus extend His comfort and help to those who have been victimized or abused?

Q3. Have you been a victim of someone else's cruelty against you? Please share your experiences.

(Coach Read)

Have you ever asked the question, "Why does God allow the innocent to suffer?" There is so much pain in the world, and everyone feels it to some extent. Sometimes people suffer as a direct consequence of their own poor decisions, sinful actions, or willful irresponsibility; in such instances, we see the truth of *"The treacherous way is their ruin." (Proverbs 13:15) ESV.*

But what about the victims of the deception? What about the harmless victims? Why would God allow such a thing to happen?

One reason could be as it says in (John 9:3) when Jesus was addressing the Pharisees about the blind man. He said it happened so that the works of God might be displayed in him. The man's blindness was not the result of personal sin; rather, God had a higher purpose for the suffering.

> God sees everything; His thoughts and ways are not ours, and His comprehension is not ours since it is higher than ours. (Isaiah 55:8-9). He reminds us that we live in a fallen world yet are not of it. (John 17:14-16). He has the ability to use our pain for a higher purpose that we cannot see or comprehend.

Another time, Jesus remarked on the deaths of some people who died in an accident: *"Do you think the eighteen who died when the tower in Siloam fell on them were more guilty than all the others living in Jerusalem?" I warn you, no! But unless you repent, you will perish as well." (Luke 13:4–5).*

In this instance, Jesus refuted the notion that tragedy and suffering are the result of personal sin. At the same time, Jesus stressed that we live in a world full of sin and its consequences and that everyone must repent.

Q4. How does God give purpose to suffering in the world, particularly for innocent individuals?

(Student Read)

This leads us to the next question of whether there is such a thing as "the innocent" in a technical sense. "All have sinned and fall short of the glory of God,"(Romans 3:23). As a result, no one is "innocent" in the sense of pure. We were all born with a sinful disposition that Adam passed down to us. And, as we've seen, everyone suffers, whether or not the suffering can be traced back to a particular personal sin.

The consequences of sin pervade everything; the world has fallen, and all of creation suffers as a result. (Romans 8:22).

Finally, God uses suffering to draw our attention away from this world and towards heaven. The Bible repeatedly exhorts us not to be consumed by the things of this world, but to look forward to the world to come. In this world, the innocent endures, but this world and everything in it will pass away; God's kingdom is eternal.

"My kingdom is not of this world," Jesus said (John 18:36), and those who follow Him do not consider the things of this life, good or bad, to be the end of the story. Even the most heinous of our sufferings "are not worth comparing with the glory that will be revealed in us." (Romans 8:18).

Could God stop someone from being victimized and experiencing suffering? Of course, and He sometimes does. However, He assures us that "all things work together for good to those who love God and are called according to His purpose." (Romans 8:28) KJV.

Suffering, even innocent suffering, is part of the "all things" that God uses to achieve His good purposes in the end. His plan is flawless, as is His character, and those who believe Him will not be disappointed.

Q5. In what ways does the Bible say that God uses suffering to guide our focus away from earthly life and towards His eternal kingdom?

(Coach Read)

One of the main repercussions of being victimized is that we can develop a victim mentality. Do you at times feel like you have no control over what's going on or like everyone is out to get you? Or do you feel like no matter what you do, bad things keep happening to you? If you often blame other people for things that happen to you or how you feel, you may have what is called a "victim mentality."

In fact, at times, you might feel like everyone is against you, including your partner, coworkers, family, and friends. Even though there may be things you can do to help fix the problem, you don't take responsibility for anything and act like you have no say in what happens. You have a "woe as me" attitude and simply feel whatever you say doesn't matter anyway.

Another thing, you might take things personally even when they are not directed at you. You might think thoughts like, "What did I do to deserve this?" You might also feel resentful a lot of the time. Most likely, you went through a hard time or went through a traumatic event, but you didn't have any ways to deal with it at the time. So, this mentality has been a way of life with no solution on how to be free from it.

As a result, you form this negative view or victim mindset. This made you think that life just happened to you and that you had no control over what happened. So, you allow yourself to have a defeated attitude or make excuses for why you act and think the way you do.

Q6. What are some indicators that a person may have developed a "victim mentality"?

Q6A. And how might this mindset have formed?

Q7. Are there any areas in your life perhaps with your parents, in your marriage, past friends, work people, or even church members where you have taken a victim mentality? How so?

BLAMING OTHERS FOR YOUR POOR CHOICES

(Student Read)

Eve had a victim mentality and her victimization happened because of her choice. *"She replied, "I heard you walking in the garden, so I hid. I was afraid because I was naked. Who told you that you were naked? the Lord God asked. Have you eaten from the tree whose fruit I commanded you not to eat? The man replied, it was the woman you gave me who gave me the fruit, and I ate it. Then the Lord God asked the woman, what have you done? " The serpent deceived me," she replied. That's why I ate it." (Genesis 3:10-13) NLT*

Eve blamed the snake right away, while Adam blamed his wife. Both of them were caught making the wrong choice. Eve would have been the kind of person who ridicules everyone and is always ready to tell you why you're wrong and why she's right. As we've already said, there are times when we are innocent and someone else abuses us, but often, other times like Eve it's because of our wrong doings and we get caught.

Eve told God, *"The devil made me do it."* *"The woman you gave me made me do it"*, Adam said. By putting the blame on other people, we avoid taking responsibility for our actions.

We can develop a victim mindset as a result of being abused by someone with evil intentions, or as a result of our own life choices. In either case, God can help set us free and bring harmony and peace into our lives.

Q8. Why do you think we blame others because of the choices we make?

LET'S TAKE A LOOK AT A FEW EXAMPLES TO HELP PUT VICTIMIZATION INTO A BETTER PERSPECTIVE

(Coach Read)

The husband feels victimized by his wife because she does not treat him with the honor and respect he believes he is entitled to. He asks his wife nicely to do something, and she says she will. But when she does what he asks, she does not do it exactly as he requests. She did what she thought was best without ever asking him his opinion or explaining why she made a different choice.

The husband questions why she didn't ask him his opinion or explain why she made a different decision. The woman becomes defensive and makes explanations for what she did. The husband feels victimized and believes his wife does not honor or respect him. This argument occurs often, and they frequently dispute over it. Both feel victimized by the other and yet they never address the real issue.

What if you were due a promotion at work and you didn't get it? Would you think that you deserved it and that your boss was out to get you? It couldn't be that he found you playing on the Internet every day instead of working. You immediately believe you are the victim, and justify in your heart, that he never liked you from the beginning and you knew it.

What if your father was a pastor, and later, you became a pastor of a church? However, when you did, you set up your church to protect yourself from the mistreatment that you witnessed the Church subjecting your father to. You genuinely believed that the way they treated him was unjust. As a result, you made a personal commitment to yourself to never allow the church to treat you in the same way. Consequently, you built emotional barriers and strived to self-protect yourself.

You structured your church in a way that eliminates any oversight from a governing board of Elders. Whenever a church leader questions your authority, you respond aggressively or cut them off completely. By prioritizing self-protection, you inadvertently prevent yourself from forming close relationships, ones where others can offer valuable advice and address difficult issues. Self-protection arises from a fear of becoming a victim and wanting to maintain control.

Someone who has implemented self-protective measures in their life has a victim mentality because they are taking responsibility and control over what they allow to happen. Whether you are a church pastor or a stay-at-home mom, experiencing victimization is something that can happen to anyone.

We can give thousands of examples of victimization, but I believe it is clear what victimization is based on these few examples. When we assign blame, we rationalize a negative internal state or challenging external situation by focusing on the wrongdoings of others.

> God does not want your victimization to turn into a mindset that affects everything that happens to you in life. He doesn't want you to spend the rest of your life wearing glasses that cast a negative light on what you have experienced in the past. God wants you to think differently. He wants you to have an overcomer mindset! He wants you to learn to deal with people and life circumstances the way He sees them.

Self-protecting oneself is not the solution to achieving freedom; it only results in adopting a lifestyle of being a victim. Instead, humble yourself under the powerful influence of God, so that He may elevate you at the right time. *You should cast all your worries and cares upon Him, for He genuinely cares for you (1 Peter 5:6-7).* God will always use your pain and suffering for your good, for He is a good God. You can trust Him with your life, allow yourself to let down the walls of victimhood, and hand over control of those aspects of your life to God.

Q9. Why is self-protection not considered an effective solution to prevent victimization?

Q9A. And what alternative approach is suggested?

DEALING WITH SHAME AND REGRET

(Student Read)

Another experience people have in this world that is hard to overcome is shame and regret. Everyone feels some sense of shame and regret for the mistakes they committed in the past. Sometimes it's something that happened to you that was outside of your control, but it still caused others pain and suffering. The Bible says a lot about shame and regret, and there are many examples of people in the Bible who have felt these negative feelings.

Can you imagine how much regret and shame Adam and Eve must have felt after they sinned? They desecrated God's creation. Adam and Eve lived in a flawless world, had everything that was made perfect, and were in perfect communion with God. When they chose to sin against God, they subjected all of God's creation to the consequences of sin, including disease, decay, death, and eternal separation from God.

Following that, every human being was born with a sinful nature and now it was natural for man to sin. Thankfully, God is sovereign, and He already had a plan in place to redeem His world via His Son, Jesus Christ, and give humans the option of salvation and eternal life with Him. But Adam and Eve must have spent the rest of their life on Earth mourning their loss of innocence and the blessings that came with it.

(Genesis 3:10) says, "that they were ashamed at their nakedness." They must have lived the rest of their lives with regret—after all, they remembered paradise and probably longed to go back to it.

> People always say God could never forgive me for what I've done. This is a lie from Satan. The Bible puts it this way: *"For God made Christ, who never sinned, to be the offering for our sin, so that we could be made right with God through Christ"* (2 Corinthians 5:21 NLT).

He can; granted, you may have to live with the consequences of your sin, but that doesn't imply God can't or won't forgive you. Think about it, arguably the most notorious serial killer (and sex offender) in modern American history, Jeffrey Dahmer became a Christian while serving out the prison sentence he received for his numerous crimes. Baptized by a local Wisconsin minister Roy Ratcliff, Dahmer revived the Christian faith he lost in his childhood before being killed by a fellow inmate at a prison in Portage, Wisconsin, in 1994.

If God can forgive Jeffrey Dahmer, he can forgive your horrible sin.

Let it go and Be Free.

Q10. How does the story of Adam and Eve illustrate the concept of shame and regret?

Q11. How does this relate to the belief that God can forgive any sin, regardless of its severity?

(Coach Read)

When we begin to mature spiritually in our relationship with God, our eyes are opened to the understanding that God has removed our sins as far as the East is from the West. (Psalm 103:12). Yes, we may regret the mistakes of our past, but they no longer govern how we live. We learn to keep our eyes fixed on Jesus, the Author and Finisher of our faith. (Hebrews 12:2).

> *"Brothers and sisters, I do not consider myself to have taken hold of [the goal] yet," Paul said. "But one thing I do is forget what has happened in the past and press on toward the goal of winning the prize for which God has called me heavenward in Christ Jesus." (Philippians 3:13–14).*

Shame and sorrow are part of the past. To be set free, we must learn to let go and trust that God has forgiven us once and for all.

We might have a dreadful history, but we have a bright future. We once walked in foolishness and rebellion, but now we walk in newness of life (Titus 3:3-7; Romans 6:4). God has forgiven the sins that we are ashamed of and the regret we feel. There is no sin too great that he cannot forgive, we can now proceed forward.

> "I have been crucified with Christ; and it is no longer I who live, but Christ lives in me; and the life which I now live in the flesh I live by faith in the Son of God, who loved me and gave Himself up for me," Paul writes in (Galatians 2:20).

Q12. What sin in your past will God not forgive?

Q12A. Is it possible to live without regret or shame, why?

A TRAGEDY THAT LEFT A FISHERMAN SUFFERING WITH GUILT AND SHAME

(Student Read)

Many years ago, in a small coastal town, lived a middle-aged fisherman named Thomas. He was well-known and respected in the community. However, Thomas held a secret that was eating him up from the inside. You see, years ago, he had been responsible for a devastating boating accident that had cost the lives of two fellow fishermen, and he had kept it a secret.

Thomas had been a young and reckless fisherman at the time. Caught in the thrill of the dangerous sea, he had ignored the warning signs of an approaching storm. He had convinced his companions they should brave the storm, asserting it would lead them to the most abundant catch. When the storm hit with its full force, the small fishing boat couldn't withstand it, resulting in the tragic loss of his friends while Thomas miraculously survived. He never let anyone know that he was on that boat.

The guilt and shame gnawed continuously at his heart. He hid the truth from everyone, enveloped in grief for his friends and regret for his momentous error. However, the weight of his secret began to affect his life and relationships. He grew distant from the community that he once cherished and the joy he found in fishing gradually faded away.

One stormy night reminiscent of the fateful day, Thomas found himself at the local church, seeking peace. To his surprise, the town's respected Pastor was there, and Thomas, looking for redemption, confessed his secret.

In the Pastor's wisdom, he said, "Thomas, the regret you bear shows your sorrow and your willingness to repent. It is the first step towards your redemption. God doesn't expect us to be perfect, only that we seek His forgiveness when we stray, grow from our mistakes, and use those lessons to serve Him and others."

Following this conversation, Thomas felt a divine nudge in his heart. The following day, he revealed his secret to the town, ready to face the consequences. Initially, there was anger and betrayal, but at the core of this tight-knit community was compassion and forgiveness.

> Inspired by the Pastor's words, Thomas decided to use his story to prevent similar tragedies. He began offering free safety sessions for the fishermen of the town. Teaching them about the importance of respecting the sea and safe fishing practices, he utilized his tragic story as a cautionary tale.
>
> Moreover, he advocated for measures that became instrumental in ensuring the safety of the fishing community, including better communication channels and upgraded safety gear. His actions and their resulting positive impact on the community honored the memory of his lost friends and, in a way, brought beauty from his past mistakes.

Throughout this transformation, Thomas continually acknowledged the grace of God that had guided him in this path of redemption. His story became a living testimony of God's power to use regret and shame for His glory, demonstrating the potential of divine forgiveness and the significant change repentance can ignite in a person's life.

Q13. What was the benefit of Thomas confessing what he did to the community?

Q13A. Do you have a shame and regret story of how God has helped you begin your journey to being set free from your past?

BIBLE EXAMPLES OF SHAME, VICTIMIZATION AND REGRET

(Coach Read)

Whether we have been victims, perpetrators, or have felt shame and regret. Our life experiences can cause us to develop hang-ups and will ultimately change us on the inside. Our daily lives are determined by how we interact with and/or perceive our circumstances. Most of us are aware that we have hang-ups or addictions, but we have no idea how to overcome them. Understanding that we have a choice between living in the "Tree of Life" or the "Tree of Knowledge of Good and Evil" can help us process what our next steps should be.

By choosing to live in the "Tree of Knowledge of Good and Evil", we will be made to feel inadequate. Our choice will allow what has happened to us to dictate how we live our lives. We will always focus our attention on ourselves and how we feel, rather than on God and His redemptive love for us. The devil wants us to be forever stuck in the world of blame and self-condemnation. God on the other hand wants us to believe that we can do all things through Christ who strengthens us. (Philippians 4:13)

We must reach a point where, regardless of what happens, we accept responsibility for our own lives. We can no longer hold anyone else responsible for the state of our relationship with God. Choosing to live in the "Tree of Life" every day is our only hope of ever truly being set free.

Jesus helps us get set free.

God does not want your victimization, shame or regrets to affect your entire life. God wants you to be set free. Jesus is the ultimate example of someone who was victimized but overcame a victim mentality. It's hard to watch the movie "The Passion of the Christ" when Jesus was beaten nearly to death.

That was only the beginning of His humiliation. They plucked out his beard. They spat at Him. He was offered vinegar to drink. They made fun of His kingship. They crowned His head with thorns. He was nailed to a cross. And Jesus was completely blameless. There was no deception, no guile, no sin of any kind in Him! If there was anyone who had a right to be a victim, it was Jesus. Yet, he humbly took on our sins for our redemption, thus making us free.

Q14. How does the story of Jesus' experience, as depicted in "The Passion of the Christ", serve as an example of overcoming victim mentality and achieving freedom from shame and regret?

(Student Read)

Jesus never felt sorry for Himself. But, instead, we see Christ at His lowest moment refusing to let His critics, accusers, and murderers bring Him down.

> (1 Peter 2:22-23), says, *"He committed no sin, neither was deceit found in His mouth. When He was reviled, He did not revile in return; when He suffered, He did not threaten, but continued entrusting Himself to Him who judges justly"*

Jesus put himself in the hands of God who judges, justly. There is no victim mentality in Jesus! Even while they were crucifying Him, he said, *"Father forgive them for they know not what they are doing." (Luke 23:34).* He is not bitter about what happened. Jesus gives us the best example of how to be an overcomer.

Jesus said "Fear not for I have overcome the world." (John 16:33). Jesus was encouraging His disciples to have faith in Him, despite the trials and tribulations they faced in a world filled with fear, doubt, and opposition. Furthermore, Jesus was reminding His followers that He had conquered the darkness and evil of this world and that we can as well.

Q15. How does Jesus' reaction to suffering and victimization inspire us to overcome our personal struggles with victim mentality and other life trials?

(Coach Read)

Talking about shame, can you imagine how the Roman Centurion, Longinus felt as he was standing there witnessing the death of Jesus? Longinus and his soldiers were eyewitnesses of the final moments of the earthly life of the Lord. These events shook the centurion's soul. Longinus believed in Christ and confessed before everyone, *"Truly this was the Son of God" (Mt. 27:54).*

> According to Church Tradition, Longinus was the soldier who pierced the side of the Crucified Savior with a spear, and received healing from an eye affliction when blood and water poured forth from the wound. Having come to believe in the Savior, the soldiers received Baptism from the apostles and decided to leave the military service. Saint Longinus left Judea to preach about Jesus Christ the Son of God in his native land (Cappadocia), and his two comrades followed him.

If God can forgive Longinus of his sin that brought him shame, He can surely forgive yours.

Not only did Jesus show us how to overcome victimization, but so did the Apostle Paul. He was thrown in jail for the cause of Christ. Acts 16:25-34 says Paul is in a cold dark damp prison cell and yet there is no complaining coming from his lips. He's not showing any self-pity, he is not angry towards those who put him there. There is no vengeance planned.

In fact, in Paul's letter to the Philippians, the major theme throughout is joy.

In that letter, what we see Paul doing is putting on the mind of Christ. And instead of being a victim, He became a survivor! He was able to overcome his victim mentality. His mindset was set on Christ and in the midst of calamity, he found himself worshiping God instead. Instead of complaining, he saw his victimization as an opportunity to further the gospel.

"But I want you to know, brethren, that the things which happened to me have actually turned out for the furtherance of the gospel, so that it has become evident to the whole palace guard, and to all the rest, that my chains are in Christ; and most of the brethren in the Lord, having become confident by my chains, are much bolder to speak the word without fear." (Philippians 1:12-14)

Q16. How did both Longinus and Apostle Paul transform their experiences of shame and victimization into opportunities for spiritual growth and spreading the word of God?

(Student Read)

Do you remember Joseph? His brothers sold him into slavery and faked his death to conceal their actions from their father (Genesis 37:18-36). Can you imagine the immense regret that his brothers must have felt?

Also, recall the incident when Joseph was serving as a slave to Potiphar and his wife falsely accused him of attempting to seduce her. When he rejected her advances, she informed her husband, who subsequently imprisoned Joseph (Genesis 39:1).

I'm confident that Joseph could have chosen to hold grudges and seek pity from others. He has been treated unfairly, and it's natural for him to have felt tempted to harbor bitterness and seek revenge.

Instead, his good character earned him the position of second in command of the land. He didn't have a victim mentality because when his father died and his brothers were afraid of him, he was more concerned with their concerns than with his own. He overcame his victim mentality.

> *"But Joseph said to them, don't be afraid. Am I in the place of God? You intended to harm me, but God intended it for good to accomplish what is now being done, the saving of many lives. So then, don't be afraid. I will provide for you and your children and he reassured them and spoke kindly to them." (Genesis 50:19-21)*

A victim mentality prevents you from doing what Joseph did for his brothers because it causes you to focus on yourself and revenge rather than the well-being of others. It is only when we can see people the way that Jesus sees them that we can be set free from a victim mentality.

Q17. How does Joseph's attitude and response towards his brothers demonstrate overcoming a victim mentality?

(Coach Read)

When we live in the "Tree of Life," we'll see other people the way God does. When someone else's sin hurts us, we can believe that God will deal with them in the right way and have hope. Don't let yourself attack them emotionally or physically. Don't let what they did hurt you, either. Just pray for them and let it go.

Let God fight your battles and live in peace. Don't let their sin rule you. God is on your side and not against you, so it's not your fault. Satan wants you to take the bait, but you shouldn't let him. Walk in the Spirit and pray that God will show them His love.

The fruit of the "Tree of Knowledge of Good and Evil" does not have the ability to transform the heart. It can give you facts and information, but it cannot give you abundant life. *"The thief comes only to steal and kill and destroy. I (Jesus) came that they may have life and have it abundantly." (John 10:10).*

A life abundant is only found in the "Tree of Life".

Whatever caused you to fall into the victim mentality thinking, it is your responsibility to break free. Whatever sin happens to you is not your responsibility, but it is a sin to cling to it and judge them without surrendering them to God. You must stop blaming and pitying yourself and take responsibility for your life. That is one of the fundamental underlying principles of the gospel. The gospel teaches us to accept responsibility. *"Therefore, each of us shall give account to God." (Rom. 14:12)*

The victim mentality says that I am too much of a victim to have to be responsible.

Teach yourself to be grateful for what you do have in life.

> *"In everything give thanks: for this is the will of God in Christ Jesus concerning you." (1 Thessalonians 5:18)* We have to understand that we have a lot to be grateful for in life. Stop complaining, and look at every circumstance as an opportunity to bring Glory to God. *"Do all things without complaining and disputing." (Philippians 2:14)*

Forgive, when you hold resentment towards another. You are bound to that person or condition by an emotional link that is stronger than steel. Forgiveness is the only way to dissolve that link and get set free.

When you forgive, you find freedom and healing from those things, so by all means, forgive. (Forgiveness is so important that in Key 7 we will spend a whole chapter on Forgiveness.)

Q18. What is the role of forgiveness in breaking free from a victim mentality?

(Student Read)

> *"Therefore, strengthen your feeble arms and weak knees. Make level paths for your feet so that the lame may not be disabled, but rather healed. Make every effort to live in peace with everyone and to be holy; without holiness no one will see the Lord. See to it that no one falls short of the grace of God and that no bitter root grows up to cause trouble and defile many."* *(Hebrews 12:12-15)*

God has given us so many promises in His Word that if we just focus on a few, he will supernaturally move us forward. He allows us to go through the valley to strengthen us, but if we continue to trust in him and his word, we will be set free from victimization, shame and regret.

Q19. What actions can you take based on Hebrews 12:12-15 to strengthen your faith, ensure peace with everyone, and maintain holiness in your life?

Q20. How can trusting in God's promises and focusing on His words help you move forward and free yourself from feelings of victimization, shame, and regret?

Prayer: Spend some time in prayer asking God to forgive you for being a victim. He will mend your broken heart and teach you to love people in their sins as he has loved you in yours.

KEY 4 FELLOWSHIP WITH GOD

Before starting today's Key 4 on 'Fellowship with God,' take a moment to reflect on your last key regarding 'Overcoming Victimization, Shame, and Regret.' Discuss how God ministered to you through that key.

(Coach Read)

I will walk about in freedom, for I have sought out your precepts. (Psalms 119:45)

We must learn to live in the "Tree of Life" if we are to enjoy genuine communion with God. Confusion and false beliefs about God and ourselves are brought on by our poor habits and hangups that we acquired while circling the "Tree of the Knowledge of Good and Evil".

We will be able to view God clearly and free of any uncertainty thanks to this crucial key "Fellowship with God".

According to (John 15:14), Jesus no longer refers to us as His servants but as His friends. He tells His disciples that He is both their God, whom they must obey and His friends, to whom He will grant power and secret knowledge. He explained to them that in order to be friends with Him, they must be connected to Him.

In John 15:5, Jesus used the image of a vine and branches to describe Himself as the vine and us as His branches. They will bear much fruit if they remain in Him, but if they separate from Him, they will be powerless.

> A friend of Jesus is granted access to God's throne room, they receive information before non-friends of Jesus do. They also are given God's grace which allows them the ability to perform miracles on earth that non-friends will never be able to do. The catch is that they must remain in fellowship with Him. It takes effort to maintain any relationship, and even more effort to maintain a very good relationship.

The best kind of relationship we could ever have is with Jesus, who is the author and finisher of our faith (Hebrews 12:2). He will always give us far more than we could ever give back. His love will always be greater than ours, and it will never end (Lamentations 3:22-24). The only thing we can ever give Him that is valuable to Him is our commitment to spending time with Him in fellowship on a daily basis.

Q1. In what ways can we strive to maintain our fellowship with Jesus on a daily basis?

Q2. Why is this commitment so valuable to God?

(Student Read)

As we progress through this curriculum, we will learn to use the "Tree of Life" thinking as a framework for the way we approach God and every situation we encounter. This will allow us to grow close to Jesus and learn to hear His voice, you will begin to find His heart for your life. His divine plan was made for your sake, not for His. He simply wants to protect you from very real danger, and He desires your success.

> *"The Lord your God is with you, the Mighty Warrior who saves. He will take great delight in you; in His love he will no longer rebuke you, but will rejoice over you with singing." (Zephaniah 3:17) NIV*

God desires for us to walk in fellowship with God and to know Him.

> *"And this is the way to have eternal life—to know you, the only true God, and Jesus Christ, the one you sent to earth." (John 17:3) NLT*

The knowledge of God that is being talked about here is not the knowledge of him that comes from nature and creation, because a person can know God in this way and not know Christ intimately. You can know God and say you believe in him, but deny him in your actions. You can say to your friends that you are friends with Jesus but have no evidence of power or fruit in your life.

Knowing God entails obeying Him and accepting His word as true. The only reason we could ever love God in the first place is because He loved us first. (1 John 4:19) With this love comes the obligation to either reject or embrace it. When we value our life choices over God's perfect will, we reject God's love.

By His shed blood, He made an unbreakable covenant with you that He would never change His mind about you. (Heb. 6:17-18) That certainty shows us how much He truly loves us; we cannot know this love unless we have fellowship with Him.

Q3. What does it mean to truly know God?

Q3A. And how is this different from merely knowing about Him?

(Coach Read)

In his book "Not a Fan" Kyle Idleman said:

> "The biggest threat to the church today is fans who call themselves Christians but aren't actually interested in following Christ. They want to be close enough to Jesus to get all the benefits, but not so close that it requires anything from them."

He went on to say;

> "Fans don't mind him doing a little touch-up work, but Jesus wants complete renovation. Fans come to Jesus thinking tune-up, but Jesus is thinking overhaul. Fans think a little makeup is fine, but Jesus is thinking makeover. Fans think a little decorating is required, but Jesus wants a complete remodel.
>
> Fans want Jesus to inspire them, but Jesus wants to interfere with their lives."

Following Jesus will cost you something, fans mistake knowledge of Jesus for true Intimacy with Jesus. Jesus doesn't expect followers to be perfect, but he does call them to be authentic. Too many Christians have a lot of knowledge about Jesus, but only a few of them can actually tell you what He said to them this morning.

Q4. What do you think is the biggest obstacle preventing Christians (You) from fully committing themselves to Jesus?

IN GOD'S PRESENCE, WE BECOME CHILDLIKE

(Student Read)

To be known by God, we must humble ourselves and enter God's kingdom like a child, (Matthew 18:3). According to (Genesis 3:17), Adam and Eve realized they were naked. Their innocence was taken away by their sin, and their fellowship with God was changed. When a child of God adjusts their life so that they are consistently in God's presence, they begin to reconnect with their innocence. They no longer have to hide from His Holiness because fellowship with Him becomes natural.

In those quiet moments with God, we will learn to converse with Him, listen to His voice, obey Him, worship Him, and enjoy His goodness. Over time, we will notice a change in our lives that reflects His characteristics, we begin to trust Him more, we become more transparent and childlike, and our vulnerability of dependence on God becomes the norm.

Adam and Eve were absolutely innocent, naked, and walking in great communion with God. They had no awareness of sin; therefore, they could not comprehend why they were fleeing from God. Everything was easy and in order since they completely trusted God with their lives. They had nothing to be embarrassed of prior to sinning, but since sinning, everything has changed.

They lost their innocent faith and started to feel burdened by feelings of guilt and shame. God never intended for us to go through this, but as a result, humanity is where it is today.

By putting concentrated effort into entering God's presence, we begin to learn how to renounce our flesh. We are able to reclaim our innocence by adopting a childlike faith when He is present. Peace and order follow, and our lives can now be changed for His glory.

Though some may mistake childlikeness for naivete or weakness, it is essentially a biblical way of life.

In (Matthew 10:16), Jesus instructs us "to be as cunning as a snake and as innocent as a dove". As we rest in God, simple innocence emerges from our friendship with God. When it comes to living our life for Jesus and His truth, we express strength and confidence just like a lion does. However, when it comes to making future decisions and living a life devoted to serving, we humbly submit to God's immense power just as a lamb does.

Q5. How was Adam and Eve's fellowship with God affected by their sin?

Q6. How does one's innocence emerge when they rest in God?

Q6A. How does this affect their strength and confidence in living their life for Jesus and His truth?

Q7. According to Matthew 10:16, what qualities do we embody when making future decisions and serving according to the guidance of God?

WHY IS A CHILDLIKE FAITH IMPORTANT?

(Coach Read)

Having childlike faith is so important in our lives because it enables us to perceive things that others are unable to perceive. It is comparable to perceiving the world through the lens of a child's imagination - everything appears fresh and attainable. It instills hope in us when everything seems lost and assists us in finding joy in everyday moments.

It serves as a reminder that we are never too old to dream. It allows us to gain insight from God's perspective. It aids in our trust in God's plan, even when we cannot comprehend it. Moreover, it grants us the courage to take leaps of faith, even when fear is present. Often, it is accompanied by other virtuous qualities, such as humility, obedience, and trustworthiness.

It allows us to perceive God's work in our lives, even during challenging times. It helps us remain focused on God rather than our circumstances, and it permits us to maintain hope even when everything seems hopeless. Faith is crucial in pleasing God, as stated in *(Hebrews 11:6) "And without faith, it is impossible to please him, for whoever would draw near to God must believe that he exists and that he rewards those who seek him."*

Q8. Why is having childlike faith considered to be important in our lives?

HAVING A CHILDLIKE FAITH TO THOSE WHO WRONGED YOU

(Student Read)

One way to determine whether or not you have childlike faith is to consider how you respond to those who have wronged you. When someone wrongs us and we react in anger or with an attitude of retaliation, this is one indication that we are not walking in a childlike faith. We are showing that we are in charge and that we will take care of the matter on our own. Managing those feelings and the need to strike out or take revenge can be quite challenging.

It's crucial to keep in mind that anger and control will only make things worse for both you and the other person. Approaching things with childlike faith and innocence requires a lot of strength, but it can also lead to calm and healing in trying circumstances. You're aware that how you react to this individual says a lot about who you are and how much control you have over your emotions and behavior.

The Bible has much to say about how we should respond to those who have wronged us. Approach the verses below as a child would when you read them. Permit your Spirit to accept them as truth, and then begin to live in accordance with God's word.

> *"But I say, do not resist an evil person! If someone slaps you on the right cheek, offer the other cheek also." If you are sued in court and your shirt is taken from you, give your coat, too. If a soldier demands that you carry his gear for a mile, carry it two miles. Give to those who ask, and don't turn away from those who want to borrow. You have heard the law that says, 'Love your neighbor and hate your enemy. But I say, love your enemies! Pray for those who persecute you!" (Matthew 5:39-44)*

And

"But to you who are willing to listen, I say, love your enemies! Do good to those who hate you. Bless those who curse you. Pray for those who hurt you. If someone slaps you on one cheek, offer the other cheek also. If someone demands your coat, offer your shirt also. Give to anyone who asks; and when things are taken away from you, don't try to get them back. Do to others as you would like them to do to you.

"If you love only those who love you, why should you get credit for that? Even sinners love those who love them! And if you do good only to those who do good to you, why should you get credit? Even sinners do that much! And if you lend money only to those who can repay you, why should you get credit?

Even sinners will lend to other sinners for a full return. "Love your enemies! Do good to them. Lend to them without expecting to be repaid. Then your reward from heaven will be very great, and you will truly be acting as children of the Most High, for He is kind to those who are unthankful and wicked. You must be compassionate, just as your Father is compassionate" (Luke 6:27-36).

Q9. How do you currently handle situations when you encounter someone who has wronged or hurt you?

Q10. What practical steps can you take to live out the principles of loving your enemies and doing good to those who hate you in your daily life?

(Coach Read)

When we are able to walk before God in our innocence, the Holy Spirit can now empower us to do God's work. In (Luke 4:18-19), Jesus stated that "*He was sent to proclaim freedom for the prisoners and sight for the blind, to set the oppressed free, and to proclaim the year of the Lord's favor*". Jesus had a childlike innocence that allowed Him to completely entrust His life to the Father.

He constantly reminded His disciples to have eyes to see and ears to hear what the Father is saying and doing. He understood that in order to be effective in His ministry, He needed to be obedient to God and faithful in His calling.

> Jesus was anointed to preach the good news; if we can walk faithfully in God's presence, we can have the same anointing that Jesus had. In the New Testament, Jesus Christ is revealed as our anointed King, Priest, and Prophet. He is God's Holy and chosen Son, the Messiah.

In fact, the term Messiah, which means "anointed one," comes from the Hebrew word for "anointed." The word Christ (Gr. Christos) also means "the anointed one."

Jesus Christ fulfilled Old Testament prophecy as the Anointed One, the chosen Messiah (Luke 4:21). He proved His anointing through the miracles He performed and the life He sacrificed as the world's Savior (Acts 10:38).

With a childlike faith and innocence, Christians today also share in an anointing through Jesus Christ. Believers receive "an anointing from the Holy One" (1 John 2:20) by sharing in the gift of the Holy Spirit (Romans 8:11). This anointing is not expressed through an outward ceremony, but through being indwelt by the Holy Spirit and joined to Christ.

As a result, we partake of His anointing (2 Corinthians 1:21-22). One scholar states that this anointing "expresses the sanctifying influences of the Holy Spirit upon Christians, who are priests and kings unto God." but through being indwelt by the Holy Spirit and joined to Christ. As a result, we partake of His anointing (2 Corinthians 1:21-22).

> One of the most powerful tools to combat the lies and attacks of Satan in your life is the anointing of God upon you. If God is on your side, no one can stand against you (Romans 8:31). By relying on God, as Jesus has taught us, we no longer rely on our own strength but on the power of God. According to (Galatians 2:20) NLT, "I have been crucified with Christ. It is no longer I who live, but Christ lives in me" (God's anointing). The life I now live in the body, I live by faith in the Son of God, who loved me and gave himself for me."

Q11. What do you believe it means to have the anointing of God?

Q11A. And what can it look like in your own life?

(Student Read)

When you have the anointing of God, you have the power of the Holy Spirit working in you. The anointing is manifested in us when we have a child-like faith in God. When we're walking in the anointing of God the darkness in the world can no longer have its way in our life. Our innocence in Jesus sets us free to have supernatural abilities that He had when He walked on earth.

> Jesus said in John 14:12 *"That all those that believe on Him, will do greater works that He did"*. Wow, that is an incredible statement by Jesus, our Innocence allows us to be empowered by the Holy Spirit to do greater works than Jesus did. That's crazy but it's true.

> According to Acts 10:38, *"God anointed Jesus of Nazareth with the Holy Spirit and with power"*. After that, Jesus went around doing good and healing everyone who was oppressed by the devil, because God was with him. Jesus believed God's word, and as a result, the Holy Spirit anointed him to do the Father's will.

We cannot force the Bible to agree with our beliefs, but we can choose to align our beliefs with the truth of the Bible, as Jesus taught us. To accomplish this, we must consume God's Word. Changing our internal truth will alter our external responses, allowing us to become more childlike.

Q12. How can one remain humble and grounded while also embracing the fullness of the Holy Spirit's power in their life?

A STORY OF A LIFE IN FELLOWSHIP WITH GOD

(Coach Read)

Hannah grew up in a broken home, causing her to develop a sense of insecurity that plagued her throughout her life. She craved approval from others to feel validated, and this led her to make poor decisions and find herself in unhealthy relationships.

One day, she decided to attend a church service with a friend, out of curiosity more than anything. However, during the worship, she felt something stir within her and she began to weep. It was as if all her pain and insecurities were being lifted off her shoulders. She knew she was experiencing the love and acceptance of God in a way she never had before.

From that moment, Hannah's life was transformed over many years. She started reading the Bible and praying every day, and her priorities slowly shifted as she sought to align her life with God's Word. Her relationships improved as she learned to value herself and others according to God's view. She began to learn that her freedom in Christ allowed her to walk in innocence before God, knowing that she was blameless in His sight.

Soon, Hannah felt a desire to serve others and advance the Kingdom of God through discipleship. Her innocence enabled her to have faith in God and His word and to have enough courage to do so. She began to mentor other women, sharing her story and the love of Jesus with them to help them find their identity and freedom in Christ. Her humility and genuine love for others was infectious, and more and more people were drawn to Jesus through her testimony.

Through the anointing power of the Holy Spirit, Hannah experienced the supernatural abilities that come with walking closely with Jesus. Miracles occurred around her, and people were healed physically and emotionally through her prayers. Yet through it all, Hannah remained grounded in her faith and humble, knowing that it was God working through her, not her own power.

Hannah's story is one of surrender, humility, and a life transformed by Jesus Christ. She saw firsthand the difference walking in innocence before God and experiencing His power can make in a person's life. Through her obedience to God's call to discipleship, Hannah helped countless others experience the same freedom and transformation that she did, ultimately advancing the Kingdom of God.

Q12. What lessons can we learn from Hannah's story about the transformative power of surrendering to God and walking in innocence before Him?

Q13. How can we apply these lessons to our own lives?

> Pray: Spend time with your leader praying aloud for God to anoint you with the power of the Holy Spirit. Repent of your sins and express to Jesus your deep desire to be blameless in His presence. Pray that God will give you the strength to stay connected to His vine (Fellowship) so that you can bear fruit for His Kingdom.

KEY 5: UNDERSTANDING OUR SPIRITUAL ORDER

Before starting today's Key 5 on 'Understanding our Spiritual Order,' take a moment to reflect on your last key regarding 'Fellowship with God.' Discuss how God ministered to you through that key.

(Coach Read)

As God's children, we all want to experience peace, joy, and happiness in our lives, just like everyone else. We don't set out seeking heartache, depression, pain, anger, and other struggles. However, even with the best intentions, we can sometimes get caught up in hang-ups that lead to bondage.

But in 1 Thessalonians 5:23, Paul reminds us that we can have God's peace and be made holy in every way, with a sense of wholeness in spirit, soul, and body, and be blameless until Jesus returns. To truly understand and receive this promise, we need to gain a better understanding of God's spiritual order.

> The story of Adam and Eve in (Genesis 2 and 3) sheds light on God's intended relationship with humanity. God promised to provide and bless them with everything they would ever need, and He hoped to fellowship with them without them ever knowing sin, evil, or anything outside of fellowship with Him.

In the Garden, the spiritual order was perfect, and because of His love for mankind, God gave them the choice to eat from the "Tree of Knowledge of Good and Evil". Before the fall, humanity lived in harmony with the Spirit of God and had the ability to make decisions that aligned with His will. However, by choosing to sin, they unknowingly disrupted the balance.

Q1. What is the significance of the "Tree of Knowledge of Good and Evil" in the spiritual order that God intended for humanity?

Q2. How did man's decision to eat from the tree disrupt the perfect spiritual order?

Q2A. And how did it lead to the hang-ups and bondages that we experience as God's children today?

CONSEQUENCE OF THE FALL

(Student Read)

It states in Genesis 3:7 *"that their eyes opened and they realized they were naked, so they sewed fig leaves together and made coverings for themselves"*. This was the moment in time when they were able to see things as God did, as stated in Genesis 3:22, where God said that *"man had become like them, knowing good and evil"*.

As a result of their actions, they were banned from the Garden of Eden and could no longer eat from the "Tree of Life". They were forced to work to support themselves, and their relationship with the Holy God was permanently altered. After eating the forbidden fruit, sin entered Adam and Eve's souls, and they now knew the difference between right and wrong, good and evil.

They immediately realized that what they did was not obediently submitting to God. As a result, they feared God and hid themselves from Him. Their connection to the Spirit was cut off, and they fell into a moral decline. Their bodies were now pressed into hard work, and they experienced heartache and pain as they searched for peace. Their spiritual order was no longer in alignment with God's will, leading them down a path that would bring chaos and destruction into their lives.

This chaos and destruction led to their son Cain killing their other son Abel, as Genesis 4 mentions. This tragic event established a worldwide system based on dominance and control. Now, every government and community is engaged in this system as a way of life. People will go to great lengths, including killing, to obtain what they desire. It's the survival of the fittest!

> There is no freedom in the world system; Going against someone else's desires will ultimately result in facing the consequences of those in power.

Q3. What are the consequences of Adam and Eve's disobedience to God?

Q3A. And how does this relate to the ways in which human society functions today?

(Coach Read)

What most individuals desire is their own version of peace, meaning, and purpose, and they will do whatever they believe is necessary to achieve it. The same goes for our personal lives, as we have all grown up and operated within this world system for our entire lives. We too seek peace, meaning, and purpose and have used methods of control and dominance according to the world's system to attain them.

Let's be honest, everything we have learned is what the world has taught us, and many of us have tried to obtain these things without God's guidance. As a result, we have developed numerous negative habits along the way that need to be unlearned. As we strive to find peace in difficult situations, we acquire layers that obstruct us from understanding God's truth.

Every decision we make that goes against God's will by attempting to control things on our own, adds another layer of callousness to our hearts and lives. These layers can bury themselves deep within us, and we may be unaware of these aspects of our lives that are out of spiritual order.

The hope we have to once again be aligned with the Father is found.

> *"I also pray for those who will believe in me through their word, Father, that they may all be one, just as you are in me and I am in you. May they be in us as well, so that the world will believe you sent me. I have given them the glory that you have given me in order for them to be one as we are one—I in them and you in me—and for them to be brought to full unity. The rest of the world will become aware that it was you who sent me, and you loved them just as much as you loved me". (John 17:21-23)*

The original sin caused a separation between humanity and God, and this is why Jesus came to save us. Being united with Jesus enables us to attain complete harmony with God, eliminating the need to conform to the ways of the world. By aligning ourselves with God, following His guidance, and embracing childlike faith, we operate in unison.

Q4. How does our individual pursuit for peace, meaning, and purpose, often governed by the world's system, impact our spiritual alignment with God?

Q5. How does the teaching of John 17:21-23 provide a solution to this issue?

(Student Read)

Many of us have gone through life without relying on God's help for a long time or have been inconsistent, and as a result, as stated before, we have developed multiple bad habits. When we face difficulties, we try to find peace by adding more layers to our lives that blind us from God's truth. Every decision we make that goes against God's perfect will adds another layer that numbs our spiritual senses.

Many of us have buried these layers so deep within ourselves, that we are unaware of those certain parts of our lives that are not in line with God's plan.

> Understanding Spiritual Order is crucial in overcoming our sinful patterns and leading a holy life that is free from anything that separates us from God.

Since we are born into a sinful world, living in harmony with God is not second nature to us. What is natural is living in the flesh. Our selfish tendencies are deeply ingrained in us. In his epistles, the apostle Paul reveals that we are in a constant internal conflict. In Romans 7:21-23, Paul explains how he struggles to do the right thing, and often ends up doing the opposite. He attributes his struggles to the sin that resides within him.

Committing sin is natural, but living a holy life is supernatural. We have the ability to sin on our own, but to live a holy life, we must seek God's help.

Q6. How can we distinguish between actions that align with God's perfect will versus those that do not?

Q7. How can we actively seek God's help to live a holy life that overcomes these challenges and brings us closer to Him?

(Coach Read)

As Paul stated in 1 Thessalonians 5:23 God created us with 3 distinct parts to our spiritual order. *"Now may the God of peace himself sanctify you completely, and may your whole spirit and soul and body be kept blameless at the coming of our Lord Jesus Christ"*. In the "Freedom" book by the Church of the Highlands, they share these three parts as such.

Three Distinct Parts to Spiritual Order

A spirit that must be redeemed

A soul that must be restored

A body that must surrender

When we surrendered our lives to Jesus, our spirit became alive in Christ and we were immediately restored to right standing with God. (Rom. 3:24) It's mind-boggling to consider that God now looks upon us as if we've never sinned. According to Paul, *"We have all sinned and fallen short of God's perfection" (Romans 3:23).*

According to the Bible, *"the wages of sin is death" (Romans 6:23)*, but because of what Christ did for us on the cross, we have been redeemed by Christ's shed blood and will no longer face eternal damnation. Our spirit has been redeemed, and we no longer fear death's sting (Romans 6:23).

In Jesus, we have been given the key that unlocks the Garden of Eden, allowing us to have fellowship with God once again, as He originally intended. However, because of our sin, we are still fighting the factors that the fall has left us with. Understanding this and living in this freedom of understanding is critical to our hope of being set free from our hang-ups.

Q8. What might living in the freedom of our redemption through Christ look like in our day-to-day lives?

\---

\---

THE SPIRIT MUST BE REDEEMED

(Student Read)

Let's unpack these three distinctives and start with the "Spirit must be redeemed". Paul shares with us in 2 Corinthians 3:16-18 *"that whenever someone turns to the Lord, the veil, or blindness from truth is taken away"*. It goes on to say *"For the Lord is the Spirit, and wherever the Spirit of the Lord is, there is freedom"*. So, all of us who have had that veil removed can see and reflect the glory of the Lord. And the Lord—who is the Spirit—makes us more and more like him as we are changed into His glorious image.

> To be set free, we must first allow God to transform us into His image, allowing us to have fellowship with Him as Adam and Eve did before the fall. We must learn to hear His voice and be led by His Spirit; how long this process takes is determined by our willingness to immerse ourselves in God's word.

God's plan for our life is that our spirit becomes the strongest part of our three-part design and be the lead in who we are and what we do. Galatians 5:16-17 says *"Walk by the Spirit, and you will not gratify the desires of the flesh. For the desires of the flesh are against the*

Spirit, and the desires of the Spirit are against the flesh, for these are opposed to each other, to keep you from doing the things you want to do."

Q9. Discuss what walking in the Spirit means.

Q9A. Can you give an example of how experiencing freedom in the Spirit can help one overcome the desires of the flesh?

(Coach Read)

As we learn to live our lives in constant fellowship with God, we will also learn to flee when temptation strikes. Our problems arise because we did not learn to rely on the Holy Spirit when the flesh was raging within us.

According to *2 Corinthians 10:5, "We must take every thought captive and make it obedient to Christ".*

> That is, do not allow negative thoughts, anxiety, depression, or feelings of hurt and pain to freely pass through your mind. With the assistance of the Holy Spirit, you must take those thoughts captive and replace them with God's word and truth.

You cannot defeat the enemy's lie without the assistance of the Holy Spirit. You now choose to *"fix your thoughts on what is true, honorable, right, pure, lovely, and admirable" (Philippians 4:8:8).* Consider things that are excellent and deserving of praise. Continue to put into practice everything you've learned and received from the Holy Spirit.

The Bible says that if we do this, *"the God of peace will be with us always" (Philippians 4:7).*

It is possible to be set free, but not in your own strength; you must learn to walk in the Spirit at all times. According to *Galatians 5:25, "if we live by the Spirit, we will also walk by the Spirit".* Make this a priority in your life from now on.

If Adam and Eve had said "No" to the serpents' temptations, they would have been free to flee from Him. When Satan attempts to deceive us into believing his lies, we now have the ability to say "NO in the Name of Jesus." Then change your location, and do something else that will bring Glory to God.

Do not stay where you are at, say "No" out loud, and remove yourself from that spot, do not stay in the trap Satan has placed in your path. We now have the tools to beat Satan's attacks because of God's word teaching us God's truth, with the Holy Spirit empowering us to be Holy, and Jesus showing us how to live in obedience to the Father.

Q10. How can relying on the Holy Spirit by taking negative thoughts captive help us overcome the enemy's lies and temptations?

Q11. How does walking in the Spirit enable us to live in obedience to the Father?

Q11A. And what can we learn from Adam and Eve's response to temptation in this context?

TO BE REDEEMED IS TO BE SEALED BY THE HOLY SPIRIT

(Student Read)

The Holy Spirit is the seal of Christians, sealing God's people. God's Spirit indwells believers! The Holy Spirit, promised to believers, identifies them as God's inheritance. The experience of the Holy Spirit in a believer's life serves as proof and a demonstration of the authenticity of their faith to both themselves and others. Additionally, the Holy Spirit provides assurance to believers that they are children of God, as we will read in Romans 8:15-16, Galatians 4:6, 2 Cor. 1:22 and Ephesians 4:30.

For you did not receive the spirit of slavery to fall back into fear, but you have received the Spirit of adoption as sons, by whom we cry, "Abba! Father!" The Spirit himself bears witness with our spirit that we are children of God. (Rom. 8:15–16)

But when the fullness of time had come, God sent forth his Son, born of woman, born under the law, to redeem those who were under the law, so that we might receive adoption as sons. And because you are sons, God has sent the Spirit of His Son into our hearts, crying, "Abba! Father!" (Gal. 4:4–6)

And who has also put his seal on us and given us his Spirit in our hearts as a guarantee. (2 Cor. 1:22)

And do not grieve the Holy Spirit of God, by whom you were sealed for the day of redemption. (Eph. 4:30)

By giving us the Holy Spirit, God seals or stamps us as His own at our conversion. And then the Holy Spirit continues to testify, authenticating the reality of this relationship by making us more and more like Jesus.

"The God who has thus authenticated this relationship will most certainly protect His people through trials and difficulties. He will do this until he takes final possession of us, His inheritance, on the day of redemption, which is at the end" (Eph. 1:14).

To be sealed with the Holy Spirit is the gracious gift of God, whereby he demonstrates the authenticity of the believer's relationship with him and his authority, ownership, and commitment to his people.

Q12. What role does the Holy Spirit play in assuring believers of their relationship with God?

Q12A. And as their status as His children, according to Romans 8:15-16 and Galatians 4:6?

A MAN THAT UNDERSTOOD THAT HE WAS SEALED BY THE HOLY SPIRIT.

(Coach Read)

In the bustling city of New York, there lived a man named Richard. Richard was a personification of a self-made, high-flying personality. He was a regular feature in Forbes magazine, shaking the business world with his extraordinary shrewdness and drive. Richard had everything he wanted: a Wall Street office with a view of the skyline, a penthouse on Fifth Avenue, and a lifestyle that many strived for, yet could hardly ever achieve.

To the people around him, Richard appeared as a man who had unraveled life's complexities. However, he remained grounded by an undercurrent of dissatisfaction and emptiness, one he couldn't quite put into words. He enjoyed the power he had, the influence, and yet it all left him still thirsting for more.

One day, on his way to a business meeting, Richard's usual self-hurried path was interrupted by a street preacher. Ordinarily, he would brush past such encounters without a second thought. But something about this preacher caught his attention. He was talking about joy, true joy that transcended the fleeting happiness of materialistic achievements—an other-worldly peace that lasts.

Out of curiosity, Richard decided to stop and listen. What was promised seemed contrarily vast to his life of singular pursuit of success. The preacher spoke of Jesus, a Savior who lovingly offered a life of true fulfillment and joy if one only gave their life over to Him.

This encounter left an indelible mark on Richard's heart. That night, Richard couldn't sleep. He spent many nights after that wrestling with his thoughts. Finally, Richard submissively gave his life to Jesus, praying for guidance and genuine fulfillment.

This decision marked a significant turning point in Richard's life. His life wasn't about accumulating wealth and social status anymore. He discovered a newfound joy, excitement, and anticipation that was incalculable to the transient happiness he once sought.

Changes did not happen overnight. Richard continued to be the successful businessman that he was. However, over time, his relationship with God became stronger and stronger, and he became more obedient to the call of Christ in his life. His pursuits became more balanced, with his faith taking on a greater significance. God became the center of his life, and he began serving in his local church and using his business skills to help others, not just for personal profit. He also made significant contributions to charities, with the goal of reducing global poverty. His life was no longer solely about himself; It became about sharing the love and grace of Christ that he had personally experienced.

With time, a light bulb went off in Richard's head, he read *2 Cor 1:22 which says "And who has also put his seal on us and given us his Spirit in our hearts as a guarantee".* This hit him in a new and profound way that he belonged to God and he was His child, the sealing of the Holy Spirit was proof and joy overwhelmed him. He could not describe this sense of spiritual family ties and the excitement it infused in him. Life took on an extra dimension of meaning and satisfaction that he couldn't translate into words—experiencing each day as a gift, every encounter as an opportunity to share this inexplicable joy.

No longer the high-flying tycoon, Richard gained a reputation as a philanthropist, dedicated servant of God, and compassionate friend to many. His old life was a stark contrast to his new life, inspiring everyone who knew him. Far greater than all of his previous accolades, was this extraordinary turn of events, reminding all, that true joy lies not in self-centered pursuits, but in living a life committed to serving others and answering to a higher calling.

Q13. What is the significance of being sealed with the Holy Spirit?

Q13A. And how does the Holy Spirit serve as proof of one's faith in Christ?

THE SOUL

(Student Read)

Our Soul must be restored after our Spirit has been redeemed. Over and over again in Scripture, people are referred to as "souls" (Exodus 31:14; Proverbs 11:30).

The human soul is that part of a person that is eternal—the part that lives on after the body dies and decays.

Jesus said, we were not to fear men, who can only kill the body, but not the soul (Matthew 10:28). God's most beautiful creation is the soul, which allows us to experience relationships and appreciate the beauty of our surroundings.

> We were created in God's image, with the ability to think, reason, and express emotions. God loved us so much that He did not create us as machines that are programmed to do whatever He wants. His desire has always been to allow us to freely choose Him and or reject Him.

Our Soul is made up of *our mind,* which allows us to think and reason, *our will,* which allows us to make choices, and *our emotions* which allows us to believe, feel, and remember. Sin and spiritual death have an impact on the entire person. Our bodies, as well as our souls, are affected by sin.

Although we all sin, some people have healthier souls than others, which makes it simpler for them to have better relationships. They take fewer risks and prefer to make smarter decisions more often than not.

An individual with an unhealthy soul is more likely to be rebellious and to take more risks. If a person with an unhealthy soul seeks counseling or even treatment from a psychologist, he or she will often find it more difficult to make changes that enhance personal relationships.

Q14. How does the health of a person's soul influence their decision-making and personal relationships?

A WOMAN WHO UNDERSTOOD THE MEANING OF THE SOUL

(Coach Read)

In the humble town of Cottonwood Falls, KS lived a lady named Dolores. Dolores was a simple woman, leading a simple life as the town's baker. She was not particularly happy nor miserably unhappy. She went about her daily life hardly noticing the beauty of the world around her, losing herself in the repetitive rhythms of kneading, baking, and selling her bread.

One day, a stranger walked into her little bakery. He had a kind face, an infectious smile, and eyes that twinkled like starlight. Dolores felt an inexplicable connection with this man. His name was Gatungo, an African preacher from Rwanda known for sharing God's word when he was in town.

> Gatungo shared with Dolores words that transformed her perspective. He spoke of how Jesus wanted us not to fear men but to guard our souls, which is the most magnificent creation of God. These spiritual words made an impression so profound on Dolores that she found herself contemplating after Gatungo left.

She realized that she had focused all her life on tangible things - the bread she baked, the money she earned, and the building she lived in. She had always been afraid of not having enough, or of men who might rob her of her livelihood. Yet, she had ignored the most beautiful creation of God - her soul.

Once she understood, Dolores began to change. She began to pray and trust in God, releasing all her fears and anxieties to Him. As she grew in her relationship with Jesus, she found herself less worried about the practicalities of life and more about nurturing and restoring her soul, strengthening her relationship with God.

She started to see the beauty of God's creation around her. She appreciated the rising sun, the fresh aroma of her bread baking, the joyous sound of children playing, and the sweet old couple that would always buy a loaf of bread shared between them. Dolores smiled more, her soul-stirring as she experienced the beauty around her.

News of her transformation spread throughout Cottonwood Falls. The townsfolk initially greeted the changes with skepticism, but they couldn't deny the peace and joy that were radiating from Dolores. They noticed how the rolls seemed warmer, the pastries tasted sweeter, and the bakery was filled with an aura of peace.

One day, a fellow townswoman named Jane, burdened by her worries, shared her troubles with Dolores. Emulating Gatungo, Dolores spoke about the teachings of Jesus, about the irrelevance of fearing men, and about cultivating and restoring one's soul. Jane, moved by her words, started her spiritual journey with Christ as well.

> And so, Dolores began to not just bake bread but to also sow the seeds of God's love in the hearts of her fellow townsmen. The humble baker woman of Cottonwood Falls became a beacon of light, illuminating the path toward spiritual growth.

Dolores' life changed remarkably when she learned that our Soul must be restored after our Spirit has been redeemed, reminding everyone of Jesus's words - we are not to fear men who can only kill the body. Through her, the people of Cottonwood Falls learned and lived the essence of God's most beautiful creation - the soul.

Q15. How does sin and spiritual death affect our souls and bodies?

Q16. Like Dolores, what steps can we take to restore our souls after our spirits have been redeemed?

(Student Read)

Personal development outside of Christ will not change a person's eternal destiny or provide him or her with a spiritual life. Similarly, a person who has become spiritually alive in Christ may still have a damaged soul that requires them to learn how to take care of their soul. Some Christians must work long and hard to break bad habits and destructive patterns.

Such struggles frequently can last the rest of their lives. The best medicine for an unhealthy soul is a healthy spirit—one that has been animated by the Holy Spirit through faith in Christ.

God is concerned with the whole person, especially the soul which can be a valid form of ministry to others. We serve *"the God of all comfort, who comforts us in all our troubles so that we can comfort those in need with the comfort we receive from God" (2 Corinthians 1:3–4). The Lord desires to change us and renew our minds (Romans 12:2).*

> *"Dear friend, I pray that you may enjoy good health and that all may go well with you, even as your soul is getting along well," John wrote in a short letter to Gaius (3 John 1:2).*

We must recognize that our free will is only truly free when it is in accordance with the truth of God's word. Otherwise, *"our souls will reap what we sow". (2 Corinthians 9:6)*

Q17. Why do you think bad habits can damage our souls?

Q18. What do you think it means to be truly free when it is in accordance with the truth of God's word?

Q19. Why is it important for Christians to take care of their souls?

(Coach Read)

"Anyone who sows to please their flesh will reap destruction, but anyone who sows to please the Spirit will reap eternal life" (Galatians 6:8). If we truly want our minds, wills, and choices to be healthy again, we must recognize that the flesh can harm our souls if we do not submit our freedoms to the power of the Holy Spirit.

Replace any negative thoughts or temptations in your mind with God's word, "Say No" out loud in the name of Jesus, and then change your location, do something different, and simply refuse to give in to your flesh with the help of the Holy Spirit.

Every individual has a life story that includes pain, whether it is the result of poor life decisions or other evil people who have hurt or harmed us. This pain has a direct impact on our spirit, soul, and body. When we face life challenges, our conscious soul steps in to help us figure out our next steps.

You feel a certain way, and your mind races with ideas for how to solve the issue or how to numb the pain. If your spirit is unhealthy and lacking in God's truth, your life choices will mirror those of the world. It will take you down a sinful path that will always lead to more heartache and pain. However, if your soul is filled with God's word and truth, you will no longer attempt to fill your soul with worldly things when circumstances arise.

You now learn to cast all your burdens on God, rest in His presence, and you train your mind to meditate on His truth.

Q20. How can we cultivate a healthy spiritual life when faced with pain and challenges?

Q21. In what ways can we actively resist the temptation to pursue fleshly desires and instead follow the guidance of the Holy Spirit?

THE BODY

(Student Read)

In order for us to be fully free, our spirit must be redeemed; our soul must be restored and our body must surrender. *Genesis 2:7 says "The Lord God formed the man from the dust of the ground. He breathed the breath of life into the man's nostrils, and the man became a living person".* This verse teaches us that God created man's body from dust, and the word "breath" (Hebrew: neshamah) refers to the spirit (Proverbs 20:27), and through these creative works, man became a living soul (Hebrew: nephesh).

The body is a person's physical structure, which includes the bones, flesh, and organs. Every cell in our bodies has its own genetic code, which is carried by a long molecule called DNA and instructs the cells on how to develop, function, grow, survive, and reproduce. We perceive the physical world through our bodies, using the five senses of sight, hearing, taste, smell, and touch.

Our bodies have both good and bad appetites. The Bible warns us to be wary of any sin that allows our flesh to get what it wants. People frequently wonder how far they can sin and still reap the benefits of God's blessing. The problem with sin is that it never satisfies; we are always looking for ways to satisfy the next craving.

Carnal desires (Set your minds on things of the flesh), cause us to crave satisfaction, and while we may satisfy them temporarily, the craving returns with increased intensity. This cycle will continue to repeat itself until we break through it with the help of the power of the Holy Spirit.

Q22. How do our bodies play a role in our awareness of the world around us?

Q22A. And our ability to experience pleasure and temptation?

Q23. How can we break the cycle of carnal desires that lead us to seek temporary satisfaction through sin?

A LADY WHO STRUGGLED WITH ADDICTIONS THAT INVOLVED HER BODY

(Coach Read)

Lydia was a kind soul, yet life dealt her more stress than joy. Whenever a disagreement erupted with her husband or tension-filled her days, she'd retreat to food for comfort. Lydia's escalating weight became a growing concern, a visible reminder of her struggles.

Seeking a solution, Lydia decided to substitute her stress-eating habit with another, arguably healthier, one. She began going to the gym. Hours would turn into days, days into weeks. Sweat and the rhythmic hum of the treadmill became her new solace. As the pounds fell away, she earned admiring looks and flattering compliments. It felt nice.

Yet, her mirror reflected a fit body masking an addict's mind. Now, instead of food, the gym was her vice. She understood that she had merely replaced one addiction with another, neither of them truly getting to the root of her issues. Lydia was at a crossroads; she felt trapped and her spirit yearned for liberation.

Having been a lifelong churchgoer, Lydia longed to feel the peace and freedom she heard spoken of in sermons. Jesus, they said, could unburden her, could give her the freedom she so desperately sought. She yearned for it, yet she was unsure, feeling helpless and hopelessly lost.

> One Sunday, after a usual hour of sweating out stress at the gym, Lydia found herself seated at the back pew of her church, tears silently staining her cheeks. She didn't want to live like this anymore. She wanted to believe, to be set free, but she didn't know how.

Seeing her distress, Pastor Andrew, a kindly man who had been guiding the Community Church for decades, walked over. He gently asked her what was troubling her soul.

Lydia opened up to him, pouring out her two-fold addiction struggle and her longing for spiritual freedom. Having served countless individuals dealing with life's many challenges, Pastor Andrew intently listened, his heart full of compassion.

He stated, "Lydia, faith is not just attending church, but a personal relationship with God. Jesus is not a magic wand to wave away problems. Instead, He offers His strength for you to overcome. You must invite Him into your struggles, pray, read His words, and ask Him 'What would you have me do, Lord?'"

He further suggested, "Your battle is not only physical; it is a spiritual one that must be fought with spiritual weapons." He spoke about the importance of viewing our bodies as God's temple and using them to bring glory and honor to Him rather than to ourselves. When you eat or go to the gym, walk in the Spirit and find balance, doing all things with the mindset of Christ. Do not engage in these activities solely due to life circumstances, but rather as an act of obedience in order to bring God glory.

Lydia took his words to heart. She began to incorporate prayer into her daily routine, not just as a plea for help, but as a moment to strengthen her relationship with Jesus, and to consult Him in her decisions. Days turned into weeks, weeks into months. There were hurdles and moments of weakness, but Lydia persevered. She began to find balance in her life, her workouts became less frantic, her meals more joyous.

Her problems didn't go away, but her learning to walk in the Spirit gave her the strength to face them. The promise of Jesus hadn't failed her - she had found her path to freedom. Lydia's journey wasn't easy, but she found hope amidst her hopelessness, and in doing so, became a testament to the transformative power of Jesus.

Q24. What significant change did Lydia make in her life to cope with her addiction struggles with her body?

Q24A. And how did it impact her?

(Student Read)

If you put your body in front of a computer screen to watch porn in order to find temporary relief from your pain, then that event will cause your eyes and body to crave more. You convince yourself that it helped once and will help again. After a while, you discover you have to have it, and your habits have led you into a pornographic addiction.

Another scenario that many people wrestle with is that you are coping with stress in your life and you discover that food, sugar, ice cream, or anything edible can help you distract yourself from the stress. We call these comfort foods, but after a while, you realize you're much heavier and your body isn't functioning as well as it used to.

Also, like Lydia maybe your addiction is working out; you go to the gym all the time to relieve tension. But are you working out to fill a void that is in your life, is it because it feeds your ego that helps fuel your pride?

God desires that our bodies be in good physical condition, but not for our own glory or to substitute Him when circumstances occur. Our bodies are to be used as tools to advance His kingdom and to do what is right.

Romans 6:13 says "Do not let any part of your body become an instrument of evil to serve sin. Instead, give yourselves completely to God, for you were dead, but now you *have a new life. So, use your whole body as an instrument to do what is right for the glory of God."*

To use your body in ways that lead to sin is to replace God's help by the Holy Spirit with your own efforts. Satan has lied to you in making you believe that it is okay to do so.

Create new habits with your body, avoid temptation, and substitute it with something that would honor God, such as worship, reading His word, or doing anything that does not put you in a vulnerable position to sin.

Q25. How can we ensure that we're using our bodies as tools to serve God's kingdom instead of feeding our addictions or filling voids with unhealthy habits?

Q26. How do we develop new habits that honor God and keep us from falling back into old patterns that lead us down the path of sin?

(Coach Read)

Do you see a pattern here? The Spirit is the most important aspect of recovery. We cannot correct our souls without the Holy Spirit's assistance, and we cannot surrender our bodies to God without the Holy Spirit's assistance.

> According to *1 Corinthians 6:12*, *"I am permitted to do anything,"* but not everything is beneficial to me. And, while *"I am free to do whatever, I must not become a slave to anything."*

The ripple effect is another real consequence of sin.

> We must learn to ask questions like, how will this action negatively affect my Spirit, Soul, and Body? How will this action negatively affect those around me? How would my action help or hurt my relationship with God? Will this action bless those around me for God's glory or will it cause someone to stumble if they catch me doing this?

If you ask yourself those questions and give honest answers, and they do not reflect God's truth, you are in serious trouble of sinning.

As Church-age believers, we are not under the law, but under grace, which means we are expected to live by a supernatural standard that can only be attained when we live for Christ, die to self, walk in spirit and truth, and submit to the leadership and guiding of the Holy Spirit.

As Christians of the Church Age, we are not bound by the Mosaic Law (and its numerous requirements) that was given to Israel as part of their covenant relationship with God. The Mosaic Law's primary goal was to identify sin and bring the offender to Christ. We are also not bound by man-made laws, religious norms, or legalistic regulations, which are all too frequently imposed by denominational churches or legalistic persons.

As Christians, we are not obligated to celebrate specific feasts, visit certain places, eat certain foods, or act in certain ways as part of our 'religion' or faith, as Israel was.

> However, we must always remember that, while everything is legal for us, not everything is practical.

As Christians, we are not obligated to follow certain forms, formulae, rites, or rituals that supposedly identify us as Christians, nor are we required to maintain ourselves 'saved' by doing so. We are not obligated to attend specific feasts or engage in specific ceremonies. We are not forbidden from participating in particular activities (such as feast days), but we are not forced to follow specific norms or perform mandatory acts in order to retain our place in Christ.

We are not subject to any type of legalism. (Legalism means when we base our justification on our own law-keeping rather than on the finished work of Christ).

Paul recognized that our liberty may cause us to be emotionally or spiritually bound and so he concludes all things are permissible for me, but I will not be brought under the authority of any such thing. The freedom we have in Christ liberates us from the constraints of legalistic rituals and religious norms, but we must be careful not to become caught in any activity that binds us - or allow it to become an obsession in our lives.

Q27. What is the significance of the Holy Spirit in the process of recovery and surrendering our bodies to God?

Q28. How does the concept of 'everything being legal for Christians' affect our daily lives and decisions?

Q29. How can we maintain our freedom in Christ while avoiding becoming emotionally or spiritually bound by legalistic rituals or religious norms?

(Student Read)

When your body is placed in a compromised situation, learn from what Joseph did in the Bible. You must run away as quickly as he did when Potiphar's wife wanted to sleep with him. Joseph used his mind to figure out what would happen if he gave in to Potiphar's wife. He knew that if he did that, it would be a sin against God and hurt his relationship with his master.

If your body is in places where it will be tempted to sin against God and other people, simply run away. To not do so will only create in you a bad habit that won't set you free in the long run; it will only continue to hurt you. We get into ruts that lead to hang-ups or addictions because we don't rely on the Holy Spirit to lift us out of our weakest moments.

In Luke 11:33-36, Jesus tells us that once we are saved for all eternity, our bodies are to be lights in the darkness, so we must be cautious about what we allow our bodies to see.

> *"No one after lighting a lamp puts it in a cellar or under a basket, but on a stand, so that those who enter may see the light. Your eye is the lamp of your body. When your eye is healthy, your whole body is full of light, but when it is bad, your body is full of darkness. Therefore, be careful lest the light in you be darkness. If then your whole body is full of light, having no part dark, it will be wholly bright, as when a lamp with its rays gives you light."*

Q30. How does Jesus say we should be cautious about what we allow our bodies to see if we are to be lights in the darkness?

Q31. Additionally, what must we do to live in Spiritual Order as God intends us to live?

Pray: Ask God to give you the strength you need to keep developing your ability to rely on the Holy Spirit at all times. To ensure that your soul and body reflect God's character rather than your own, ask Him to show you the proper ways to discipline them. Ask God to set you free from any bondages that are currently in your life, that are preventing you from experiencing true freedom.

KEY 6: WHAT DO WE VALUE MOST

(Student Read)

In Luke 14:33, "Jesus stated that we cannot be His disciples unless we give up everything we own to Him". A disciple is a Christ-follower who "practices disciplines" in the way they live out their lives.

According to Exodus 34:14, *"God is a jealous God who will not compete with any other Idol in your life"*. As disciplined followers of Christ, we must do everything in our power to eliminate any other distractions in our lives that might keep us from having a close relationship with Him. Two of the biggest distractions can be the pursuit of material wealth and relationships.

Paul said in *1 Corinthians 9:27, "I discipline my body like an athlete, training it to do what it should. Otherwise, I fear that after preaching to others I myself might be disqualified"*. If we want our Spirit, Soul, and Body to walk in spiritual order, we must first determine in our hearts that God comes first and then do everything with the Holy Spirit's power to ensure this is the case.

Q1. What does Luke 14:33 convey about the requirement of becoming a disciple of Jesus?

Q1A. And how does it align with Paul's message in 1 Corinthians 9:27 about self-discipline?

MATERIALISM

(Coach Read)

The desire for the things of this world is a major temptation that keeps Christians from disciplining their bodies as athletes. This is referred to as Materialism, which is defined as (the preoccupation with material things rather than intellectual or spiritual things). It is clearly wrong for a Christian to be preoccupied with material things.

That is not to say we cannot have material possessions; however, the obsession with acquiring and caring for "stuff" is dangerous for the Christian for two reasons.

First reason: any preoccupation, obsession, or fascination with anything other than God is sinful and displeases God. We are to *"love the Lord, your God, with all your heart, soul, and might" (Deuteronomy 6:5)*, which is the first and greatest commandment, according to Jesus (Matthew 22:37-38).

As a result, God is the only thing we can (and should) habitually occupy ourselves with. He alone is deserving of our undivided attention, love, and service. To offer these things to anything, or anyone, else is idolatry.

Second reason: when we are concerned with the material world, we are easily drawn in by the "deceitfulness of wealth" (Mark 4:19)

Believing that if we only had more of whatever it is we are chasing, we would be happy, fulfilled, or content. This is a lie from Satan, the father of lies. He wants us to chase after something he knows will never satisfy us in order to keep us from pursuing the only thing that can satisfy us—God Himself. According to Luke 16:13, *"We cannot serve both God and money."*

We must strive to be content with what we have, and materialism is the polar opposite of that. It drives us to strive for more and more while telling us that this will be the answer to all of our needs and dreams. According to the Bible, a person's *"life is not in the abundance of his possessions" (Luke 12:15)*, and we are to *"seek first the kingdom of God and His righteousness" (Matthew 6:33)*.

> **Being CONTENT with your life means that you're satisfied with where God has placed you.**
>
> Instead of comparing yourself to others or wishing you had a different life, you are at peace living a life with purpose for God's glory. You accept the giftings God has given you and learn

to thrive in them every day. You have an attitude of thankfulness and see life from Christ's perspective.

"Now there is great gain in godliness with contentment, for we brought nothing into the world, and we cannot take anything out of the world. But if we have food and clothing, with these we will be content". (1 Timothy 6:6-8)

Rather than wish that things could be different or resent how your life is going, being content with your life means you trust God and allow Him to lead your next steps in His timing.

Q2. What are the two main reasons mentioned for why an obsession with material possessions is considered dangerous for Christians?

Q3. How does CONTENTMENT contrast with this?

Q3A. Describe what your life would be like if you lived contently.

A GUY THAT COLLECTED AIR JORDANS SHOES

(Student Read)

Ethan was renowned for his extravagant lifestyle and his particular obsession with Air Jordan shoes.

Ethan was not a wealthy person but still managed to collect hundreds of Air Jordan shoes. As a child, he hailed from humble beginnings. Although his family was far from affluent, he had a passion for basketball. He idolized Michael Jordan and dreamed of owning pairs of the coveted Air Jordan sneakers that Jordan wore on the court. When Ethan grew older and established a somewhat successful career, he found himself in a position to afford not just one, but over time many pairs of Jordans.

His collection started with just one pair. But soon, one grew into a dozen, a dozen quickly became fifty, and before he realized it, Ethan had accumulated over three hundred pairs of Jordans. His apartment, a monument to his obsession, was overtaken by towers of shoeboxes. Friends began to notice, calling him out on his excessive spending on shoes.

Ethan believed that these collections added value to his life. They served as a trophy, evidence of his hard work. They made him feel fulfilled and accomplished, and every new addition brought him a temporary surge of happiness and pride.

But soon, the thrill faded, and he began to ask himself, why? Why do I need all of these shoes, what does this say about myself? He realized he was on a never-ending chase, always desiring the newest models and limited editions. His love for Jordans had grown into an uncontrollable obsession, a kind of idol with a shameless demand for attention and money. His social life dwindled, his professional life was hindered, and his spiritual journey was halted, all due to his unquenchable thirst for material possessions.

> One day, while sitting amidst his amassed collection, Ethan felt a deep sense of emptiness. This wasn't the life he wanted. He remembered his youthful aspiration of becoming a helpful, contributing member of society, not just a man ruled by his desire for material wealth. He realized his fixation was a distraction, an idol that competed with his relationship with God.

It was a difficult internal battle, but Ethan decided to emulate the self-discipline spoken of by Paul in 1 Corinthians 9:27. With a resolute heart, he began to prune his life, step by step, starting with his expansive shoe collection.

He sold most of his Air Jordans, using a portion of the proceeds to support ministries that advanced God's kingdom, and only kept a few pairs for himself. He pursued a more minimalist and non-materialistic lifestyle, focusing more on his spiritual growth and rekindling his relationship with God.

The path was not easy; it demanded commitment, contentment, perseverance, and discipline. However, Ethan found freedom in putting God first, feeling more fulfilled than he ever did amid his hundreds of Jordans. The transformation was tremendous, not just materially, but spiritually, as Ethan became a true disciple, putting God first in everything he undertook.

Q4. What prompted Ethan to reconsider his obsession with collecting Air Jordan shoes?

Q4A. And how did this realization affect his life?

(Coach Read)

What material desires do you think about most when you close your eyes at night? Do you ever meditate on how to get ahead in your life or how to make more money? How about making plans for your next big trip, getting high, your next drink, getting a new car, etc?

When things are quiet and we have time to think about what we really care about, we can always tell where our hearts and temptations are.

Jesus wants us to care about things that will last forever, *"Do not store up for yourselves treasures on earth, where moths and vermin destroy, and where thieves break in and steal. But store up for yourselves treasures in heaven, where moths and vermin do not destroy, and where thieves do not break in and steal. For where your treasure is, there your heart will be also". (Mathew 6:19-21)*

When we get to heaven, we will have all the wealth we want. Let's keep our eyes on Jesus while we're on earth and see the world the way He does. We don't have time to think about how to get rich because all we can think about is how to work with God to advance His kingdom.

If God makes you rich, it's the byproduct of His goodness but it's not because you made it your main priority. He is to be your priority and He takes care of the good things in your life.

As Paul teaches us in Philippians 4:11-13 We learn to be content, to rest in where God has us, and follow Him. *"Not that I am speaking of being in need, for I have learned in whatever situation I am to be content. I know how to be brought low, and I know how to abound. In any and every circumstance, I have learned the secret of facing plenty and hunger, abundance and need. I can do all things through him who strengthens me."*

Q5. What does Matthew 6:19-21 suggest about our focus on material wealth?

Q6. How is this perspective reflected in the teachings of Paul in Philippians 4:11-13?

Q7. Ask yourself, has God revealed to you anything in your life that is more important than Him?

RELATIONSHIPS

(Student Read)

Every relationship has its ups and downs. A relationship takes work, whether we've known each other for a week or five decades. Many of those ups and downs can cause your relationships to come between you and God. Not only with your partner, but also with family, friends, coworkers, pastors, church members, neighbors, and even enemies.

If you are not careful, you can begin to put more value in your relationships than you value your relationship with God.

We tend to perceive our relationships in physical terms; we aspire to be more emotionally involved and desire our partnerships to fill a void within us. When our relationships don't meet our needs as we believe they should, we often insist on getting our own way. In an attempt to control the outcome, we begin to discuss with them how we feel and what we desire.

If this is done in our flesh and not under the guidance of the Holy Spirit, it will cause problems in the relationship. This perspective will eventually hurt the relationship and cause us to lose sight of God. When we become the god of our relationships, acting as if we know what is best instead of submitting them to God, our lives can swiftly slide downward.

Q8. What are the potential consequences if we place too much value on our earthly relationships over our relationship with God?

Q9. How does it affect our interactions and emotions when our relationships don't meet our expected needs?

TOXIC RELATIONSHIPS

(Coach Read)

The fact that marriage is the most intimate relationship that two individuals can have, outside of their relationship with God, does not come as a surprise. Interestingly, marriage has the ability to bring out both the best and the worst in people, as two separate individuals strive to live as one flesh.

It is important to acknowledge that selfishness lies at the core of most marital issues. In other words, when one or both partners prioritize their own needs above all else, conflicts are likely to arise. If your bond is solely based on physical attraction, or what you can get from the marriage it will not bring freedom into your lives; Instead, you will find yourself trapped.

It can even lead the marriage into a toxic relationship. Such a toxic relationship may require the couple to separate from each other for a period of time until both individuals can strengthen their relationship with God and find healing in His presence. Only after that should a couple consider reconciling the marriage if it has become toxic. Staying together during this time does not benefit your relationship with the Lord." The only way to find freedom in your relationship with your spouse is by having God be the most important part of your marriage.

Likewise, if you have friendships with people where the relationship has become toxic, it would be wise to end those friendships or distance yourself from them. You should never let Satan convince you that your relationship with your friend is more important than your relationship with God.

It is crucial to remove yourself from any toxic relationship that causes harm to you and, most importantly, harm to your relationship with God. Especially if that relationship is abusive and is causing physical harm to you.

A toxic relationship is one that makes you feel unsupported, misunderstood, demeaned, or attacked. A relationship is toxic when your well-being is threatened in some way—emotionally, psychologically, and even physically.

Q10. How does prioritizing God in a marriage or friendship contribute to strengthening the relationship?

Q10A. And how does it help reduce the likelihood of it becoming toxic?

A TOXIC MARRIAGE RELATIONSHIP

(Coach Read)

Both Sam and Martha were devout Christians and met in their local church's youth group. There was a sweet simplicity to their love, woven with shared values and faith. However, years into their marriage, their relationship started showing signs of strain. Soon, the sweetness turned bitter, their togetherness started to feel lonely.

Sam and Martha were both involved in serving at Church, but selfishness began creeping into their lives. They began to demand more from each other, often letting their personal desires overshadow their love and respect. Their expectations grew tall, often eclipsing the sanctity of their vows, leading to a toxic atmosphere at home.

Their interactions turned into a battlefield, filled with aggressive confrontations. There was an overt imbalance of power; Sam, more assertive by nature, dominated most of their decisions. Martha, quieter yet not submissive, started harboring resentment. Sam rarely took responsibility for the tension, always blaming Martha for their disunity. They found constant fault in each other, frequently fought over trivial issues, and demanded their way without regard for the other's feelings.

Such toxicity robbed them of their joy and peace and their kids' lives were being influenced by all the fighting. Both started to feel drained, exhausted, and lacking the strength even to pray together. It was suffering neither had anticipated, and they questioned why their faith was not aiding peace in their relationship.

Their pastor, a wise old man, had been observing them for a while. Aware of how bad the toxicity was consuming Sam and Martha, he decided to intervene. He called them one evening and suggested they take some time apart.

> **"This isn't about surrender," he told them gently, "It's not about accepting defeat but about building strength — strength that comes from drawing closer to God. You've let worldly desires dictate your lives for too long. Now, it's time for God."**

Initially, Sam and Martha reacted with shock and anger. But with time, they started to see the wisdom in the Pastor's advice. They agreed to separate temporarily to focus on their individual spiritual growth and learn to hear God again.

During the time they spent apart, both of them humbled themselves before God and started meeting with their Pastor and his wife for counseling. They confessed their sins before God and began realizing the significance of selflessness in marriage, seeking God's guidance to identify the areas in which they needed to make changes.

The break proved to be transformative. After they confessed their sins to one another and forgave each other, it made them realize how their selfishness had turned their sacred bond into a battleground. They understood that it was their own sins that had brought them to this point and, with God's guidance, they learned to accept responsibility for their actions, show empathy towards each other, and restore the balance of power.

After a period of separation, they returned to their relationship with a refreshed perspective. The toxicity had diminished, replaced by an understanding and respect born from their mutual growth. This time, their love felt more evolved and closer to God.

Q11. What solutions were suggested and implemented to solve the issues of selfishness and power imbalance in Sam and Martha's relationship?

Q12. How did their toxic relationship get in the way of their relationship with God?

(Student Read)

A marriage should always try to save itself because God hates divorce (Malachi 2:16). However, if divorce does occur, it is because one or both of the partners refused to humble themselves before God and reconcile. Before real reconciliation is possible, both parties must be accountable to God and choose to draw close to God in order to change themselves. Pointing the finger at our spouse or a friend will not fix the problem.

However, falling to our knees and surrendering our lives to God can and will help in the process of healing. You personally make the decision to be holy, to cease pointing fingers, and to let God take control. God can bring even the most broken relationships back together, but only if you fully surrender your life to Him first. Trust God with your partner, focus only on your relationship with God, and be obedient to His leading.

If you have a problem in your relationship, it means that Satan has deceived you at some point. He has made you believe things that are not true. You are not what Satan says you are; you are a beloved child of God. You should not believe the negative things your partner or friends say about you. The Bible says *"You are chosen, loved by God and a royal priesthood" (1 Peter 2:9)*. Satan hates you and desires to destroy you but God deeply wishes to bless you exceedingly abundantly more than you can think or imagine (Ephesians 3:20).

Stop believing the lies that have led you to where you are now. God is good and everything about Him is perfect. Seek and pursue the truth of God, and you will become free from the negative impact that relationships can have on you. Cease from being negative about everything, and surrender everything to God. Position yourself to be still and in the presence of God every day.

(Some relationships will need a professional Christian counselor to help walk with them as they learn to draw closer to God. We highly recommend you do so if God is leading you down this path).

Q13. Do I have relationships that have come between God and me? If so, what is your next step in that relationship?

Q14. How can you start aligning your perspective with God's truth and surrendering more aspects of your life and relationships to Him?

HAVE SPIRITUAL EYES TO SEE AND SPIRITUAL EARS TO HEAR

(Coach Read)

At the end of a difficult saying or parable, Jesus refers to those who have "ears to hear" in the Gospels. (Matthew 11:15; Mark 4:9, 23) Whenever Jesus says, "He who has ears to hear, let him hear," He is calling for people to pay careful attention.

It's another way of saying, "Listen up! What I have to say is very important!" But His words would be meaningless unless they were willing to tune out other distractions and come to

Jesus to understand the meaning of His preaching. They needed more than just ears, no matter how sensitive they were; they needed spiritual ears to hear and spiritual eyes to see.

God wants us to see our relationships through His eyes. He is madly in love with each of them and longs to be with each of them, even the hardest of people. When Jesus spoke to His disciples, He was always teaching them to see with their eyes and hear with their ears. He wanted them to understand that what we see and hear from the Father influences how we live.

If we walk in fellowship with the Spirit, we will learn to see and hear what the Father desires for our lives. If we approach our relationships without seeing them through God's eyes or hearing them through God's ears, we will lose sight of what the Father's perfect will is.

What if you gave up your right to be right and instead chose to be unoffended, no matter the situation?

> *"For the sake of Christ, then, I am content with weaknesses, insults, hardships, persecutions, and calamities. For when I am weak, then I am strong". (2 Corinthians 12:10)*

What if you put more value in your relationship with God by choosing to elevate your relationships above yourself, signifying you trust God more than your relationship?

> *"Don't be selfish; don't try to impress others. Be humble, thinking of others as better than yourselves". (Philippians 2:3)*

When we value God above our relationships, we demonstrate to others and ourselves that we want to trust God and believe in our hearts that He is in control.

> *"Humble yourselves, therefore, under God's mighty hand, that he may lift you up in due time". (1 Peter 5:6)*

This also will lead us to have peace in our relationship. *"Be completely humble and gentle; be patient, bearing with one another in love. Make every effort to keep the unity of the Spirit through the bond of peace". (Ephesians 4:2-3)*

Q15. How would your relationships transform if you truly saw and valued them through God's perspective, choosing humility and peace over your own rights and impressions?

(Student Read)

In order to see people through God's eyes it will require effort and discipline in how you walk in daily fellowship with Him. If you do not value God more than your material wealth or your relationships, you will be prone to bad habits, hang-ups, and addictions that will lead you to despair. Material wealth will never satisfy your spirit, and no relationship will ever be as fulfilling as your relationship with God.

Most of our problems stem from these two major factors, and unless they are surrendered to God, you will not be able to be set free from the strongholds they have over you.

It is critical that you make changes in these two areas immediately following your talk with your coach today. Do not put off adjusting what needs to be adjusted; instead, do the difficult thing and take the next move toward freedom. Don't let material desires or bad relationships stand in the way of your relationship with God any longer.

If that means selling things that have gotten in between you and God, then do it. If that means confessing your sins to a friend or spouse then do it. If you have not humbled yourself and need to, this is the perfect time to do so.

In our quest to be set free, we must make bold and necessary sacrifices. If that means selling things that have gotten in between you and God, then do it, for material possessions must not obstruct one's relationship with God. If that means confessing your sins to a friend or spouse then do it, as transparency and honesty can bring absolution. If you have not humbled yourself and need to, this is the perfect time to do so - humility softens hearts and opens the pathway for growth and personal development.

Q16. Ask and answer this hard question: Have you given God control over your money, relationships, and future?

Q17. What immediate steps can you take to be aligned with God in what you should value most?

Pray: Ask God to show you the people you need to forgive and make things right with. Ask Him to show you where your love of things has made you trust them more than Him. Share with God your heart's desire to love Him more than anything else in the world.

CHAPTER

7

KEY 7: FORGIVENESS

(Coach Read)

We've all had someone do or say something to us that has hurt us at some point in our lives, as we covered in Key 3 Overcoming Victimization, Shame, and Regret. It could be a mean-spirited comment made by someone, or they could have physically harmed you. The bottom line is that you have been hurt and are vulnerable to harboring resentment and bitterness in your heart.

Many times, we have unforgiveness and or bitterness in our hearts and are unaware of it until someone points it out to us. Failure to address this immediately may be a major factor in Satan gaining a foothold in your life, preventing you from breaking free from sins that have a strong hold over you.

An unforgiven offense is a poison to your body; it eats away at you and eventually consumes you. Over time, your decision-making will change, and walls of self-protection will begin to rise in various areas of your life. Unforgiveness and bitterness gradually erode your joy to the point where you become a prisoner of your own self-will.

It will paralyze your ability to live, to love, and to be loved. Not forgiving someone causes more harm to ourselves than it causes harm to the people we are not forgiving.

Unforgiveness also prevents us from living the full life that God intends for us. Instead of promoting justice, our unforgiveness breeds bitterness.

> *"Make every effort to live in peace with everyone and to be holy; without holiness, no one will see the Lord," (Hebrews 12:14-15).*

If we are harboring unforgiveness in our hearts, our lives will struggle to live in peace with everyone.

Q1. How can we recognize and address the unforgiveness and bitterness in our hearts?

Q2. What steps can we take to prevent such feelings from obstructing our spiritual growth?

Q2A. And our ability to live in peace with everyone?

(Student Read)

How can you tell if you have unforgiveness/self-protection in your heart?

1. You might experience bursts of anger, you bottle up your emotions and then explode.

2. You have become petty and impulsive, when interacting with people you make snide remarks or send passive-aggressive texts.

3. You are desperate to make people understand how you feel, you say things like, "If you only understand what I have been through," or "If you just knew what I had to do, and so on".

4. You make impulsive decisions, you can't control hurting people, you make unnecessary purchases, and maybe it involves comfort eating.

5. You're not taking responsibility for your feelings, you're blaming others and pretty much anything.

6. You get sick a lot, withholding forgiveness can actually make you sick.

7. You keep a list of offenses against you.

8. You simply hate yourself and others around you.

9. You gossip about people who have harmed you,

10. The final possibility is that you replay in your mind the offense someone has committed against you. You find yourself fixating so much on the past that you've allowed it to define everything you do.

Q3. What signs of unforgiveness/self-protection symptoms do I currently demonstrate in my life?

Q4. Who, if anyone, are you harboring unforgiveness against, that has hurt you?

(Coach Read)

Forgiving will never make a wrong right, but we should never hold sins against others. The hurt, pain, and memory may still be there, but even if someone does not apologize, we must release them so we ourselves are not in bondage. Prison is a depressing place to be.

Many Christians are imprisoned by unforgiveness. Even when the abuser repents, the abused continues to carry the pain. Only Jesus can heal our wounds and grant us the grace to truly forgive (Psalm 147:3). We've all offended at some point, and in the end, we've all pierced and hurt God's Son.

> A Christian brother in the Lord once said, "I remember when I was a younger believer in the Lord. Having just experienced the forgiveness and life offered in Jesus Christ and spending many hours in prayer in relationship with the Lord, everything seemed so well.
>
> I spent months in my room reading the Word of God and simply enjoying the Lord. When I came across a forgiveness passage, I really thought hard about whether I had any unforgiveness towards anyone, and I didn't.
>
> Then I thought to myself, "How could anyone harbor ill will toward them when Jesus has forgiven us all of our ill will toward Him, and nothing compares to that?
>
> Since then, I've struggled to forgive a few times, but I've always realized that I have no reason to hold anything against anyone because God forgives me. Sin against man is forgivable, but sin against the Holy Creator of the universe is unacceptable."

Q5. What steps can we take to overcome the challenge of unforgiveness?

Q6. What lessons can we draw from understanding that sin against God is far greater than any sin against fellow human beings?

(Student Read)

The Bible says a lot about forgiveness and unforgiveness. The parable of the Unforgiving Debtor, recorded in (Matthew 25:18-35), is perhaps the most well-known teaching on un-forgiveness.

> Then Peter came up and said to him, "Lord, how often will my brother sin against me, and I forgive him? As many as seven times?" Jesus said to him, "I do not say to you seven times, but seventy-seven times.

> "Therefore, the kingdom of heaven may be compared to a king who wished to settle accounts with his servants. When he began to settle, one was brought to him who owed him ten thousand talents. And since he could not pay, his master ordered him to be sold, with his wife and children and all that he had, and payment to be made.

> So, the servant fell on his knees, imploring him, 'Have patience with me, and I will pay you everything.' And out of pity for him, the master of that servant released him and forgave him the debt. But when that same servant went out, he found one of his fellow servants who owed him a hundred denarii, and seizing him, he began to choke him, saying, 'Pay what you owe.'

So, his fellow servant fell down and pleaded with him, 'Have patience with me, and I will pay you.' He refused and went and put him in prison until he should pay the debt. When his fellow servants saw what had taken place, they were greatly distressed, and they went and reported to their master all that had taken place.

Then his master summoned him and said to him, 'You wicked servant! I forgave you all that debt because you pleaded with me. And should not you have had mercy on your fellow servant, as I had mercy on you?' And in anger his master delivered him to the jailers, until he should pay all his debt. So also, my heavenly Father will do to every one of you, if you do not forgive your brother from your heart."

Q7. How does the parable of the Unforgiving Debtor illustrate the significance of forgiveness?

Q8. What implications does it have for our understanding of God's expectations of us when dealing with others who have wronged us?

(Coach Read)

Jesus informed Peter that He must forgive 490 times per day. That's forgiving someone every three minutes! Given how frequently our minds race, that number doesn't appear to be implausible, does it?

In the Parable of the Unforgiving Debtor, the first guy owed the king millions of dollars, but when he asked for forgiveness, the loan was forgiven. As sinners, we too owed a substantial debt that we were unable to repay. But God showed us tremendous mercy by paying up our debt in full through the blood of Jesus. We have been forgiven much.

The second individual owed the first individual thousands of dollars. This is not a small amount of money, but the first man had a far larger debt canceled. Given the extraordinary charity extended to him by the king, he should have readily shown mercy to the second guy. Since we have experienced so much forgiveness, we should extend the same to others. The forgiven must forgive!

> When we have been betrayed, wrongly accused, rejected, mistreated, and humiliated. Recall that Jesus was betrayed by Judas, wrongly accused by the courts, rejected by Peter, mistreated and beaten by the soldiers, and publicly humiliated on the cross.
>
> Jesus experienced all of these transgressions in a human form so that He could comprehend every difficulty we would face. Today, when we approach Him with our hurts, He can honestly respond, "I understand, I've been there too."

Not only is Jesus now able to empathize with our suffering, but He was also able to offer an example of how we should respond when we suffer at the hands of others because He went through these hardships.

Jesus asked the Father at His death to forgive those who had cursed Him and nailed His hands and feet to the cross, by saying, "They have no idea what they are doing" (Luke 23:34)

In actuality, they knew precisely what they were doing when they murdered a guy they despised and ensured he felt every ounce of their hatred.

Jesus understood that the oppressors were blinded by hatred, but He chose to see their deeds from a heavenly perspective. Offenses will inevitably occur, so we must arm ourselves with Jesus' way of thinking.

When we begin to see others as God does, we will love them like Jesus did, regardless of what they do to us.

Q9. How can adopting Jesus' perspective on forgiveness, assist us in forgiving others more quickly?

Q10. How does this perspective empower us to love others unconditionally, despite their actions toward us?

(Student Read)

One of the main reasons we don't forgive someone who has hurt us is that we don't believe it's fair to let them off the hook. We convince ourselves that they do not deserve our forgiveness.

But God does not follow the logic of fairness, which is a good thing because none of us deserve to be forgiven by Jesus. If we are to be set free from the shackles of unforgiveness, we must first recognize our own flaws.

> *"Because we have all sinned and fall short of God's glory". (Romans 3:23)*

The next step is to keep our focus on the real enemy. The devil is the enemy, not people.

> *"For our struggle is not against flesh and blood, but against the rulers, against the authorities, against the powers of this dark world and against the spiritual forces of evil in the heavenly realm." (Ephesians 6:12)*

Jesus chose to see people as people who were blinded by their own hatred and were unaware of His love. Our approach should be to love people while despising the devil.

> *"Be alert; your adversary, the devil, prowls around like a roaring lion, looking for someone to devour". (1 Peter 5:8)*

Finally, you must genuinely embrace God's love in your heart. It has been repeated many times that God loves you intensely and does not condemn you. Your sins have been forgiven, and His grace is sufficient for your life. He loves you unconditionally, and there is no action that you can do that will alter this reality. By wholeheartedly believing in this, you will gain the ability to love others.

If we are constantly struggling to love others, it is possible that we have not fully received God's love.

"Not that we have loved God, but that He has loved us and sent His Son to be the propitiation for our sins". (1 John 4:10)

Q11. How can recognizing our own flaws and focusing on the real enemy, help us to overcome the resistance to forgive others?

Q12. How does genuinely embracing God's unconditional love prepare us to better love others?

Q13. What does it imply if we are still struggling to extend that love to others as mentioned in 1 John 4:10?

FORGIVE YOURSELF

(Coach Read)

There are times in our lives when we can find ourselves too easy on ourselves, we justify our actions, and at times, we can be too hard on ourselves and condemn ourselves for everything we do.

Both Paul and Jeremiah talked about this clash between how we see ourselves and how things really are. Paul talks about pride in people, saying that we are all basically to blame (Romans 3:23) and that we tend to think too highly of ourselves (Romans 12:3). Jeremiah, on the other hand, says that it's easy for us to lie to ourselves, but only God knows the truth about what's inside us (Jeremiah 17:9–10).

To be set free we must forgive ourselves, even though self-righteousness is common, people often blame and hate themselves too much, even though God has forgiven them for their sins (2 Corinthians 2:6–8). Most people who struggle with this have trouble forgiving themselves for their past sins. John, on the other hand, gives an amazing promise: *"If we*

> *confess our sins, God's faithfulness and justice guarantee that we will be forgiven and made clean" (1 John 1:9).*

The principle of forgiving ourselves finds its roots in God's love and compassion for us through Christ Jesus (Ephesians 4:32)! Those who find themselves in Jesus are set free from self-condemnation (Romans 8:1) as well as empowered to love (Galatians 5:13). Our purpose as sinners, who have experienced the grace of forgiveness is to internalize and manifest God's mercies to ourselves and to others (1 Timothy 1:15-16)!

Those fortunate enough to accept God's grace and kindness are then transformed into beings who can extend such tenderness and grace to themselves and others. This softness is the work of God's divine power which sets us free from the potency of sin, and the persecution of evil against us (Galatians 5:1).

Emphasizing this truth, Jesus expressed, *"If the Son sets you free you are free indeed"! (John 8:36)* Embracing God's forgiveness becomes the initial step towards forgiving ourselves.

> Why is it so hard for us to let ourselves off the hook? "How can I forgive myself for hurting someone?" We may also ask "How can I forgive myself for making a mistake or making so many bad choices?"

A warning siren should always go off in your head if you have ever said, I can't forgive myself. The truth is you won't forgive yourself as long as you believe you can't. In other words, our beliefs shape our thoughts, emotions, and behaviors. The best way to change our mindset about self-forgiveness is to better understand and accept what the Bible says about forgiveness.

If you do not choose self-forgiveness, you will most likely experience regret and self-hatred (which can lead to depression). In other words, you're beating yourself up for past mistakes that Christ has already forgiven you for.

Q14. How can we find freedom in forgiving ourselves, despite the common struggles of self-righteousness and self-blame?

Q15. How can we find forgiveness for hurting someone or making mistakes and bad choices?

(Student Read)

Without self-forgiveness, you will continue to replay the tape of what you said or did, compounding feelings of shame, guilt, sadness, regret, and so on. Forgiving yourself can lead to a happier and healthier life. Your energy will no longer be depleted by memories of the past. Most importantly, you will experience the freedom that God intended and planned for your life.

"You will be truly free if the Son sets you free". (John 8:36) This is a real promise that we can put all of our hope in.

The initial step in forgiving oneself is to have an accurate perception of yourself and of God. The most effective strategy to clarify our vision is to examine what the Bible says about self-forgiveness.

"But God displays his own love for us by the fact that Christ died for us while we were still sinners". (Romans 5:8)

This means that out of his great love for every one of us, God sent Christ to die on our behalf so that we may be forgiven and redeemed. God never intended for us to achieve perfection. In fact, He anticipated that we would not properly get it right (insert Christ). Perfection is not a requirement to achieve God's love and acceptance.

We were not forgiven for doing the right thing. We are forgiven solely because of Jesus and Him doing the right thing.

Q16. How does self-forgiveness contribute to healthier and happier living?

Q17. According to Romans 5:8, how does understanding God's display of love play a pivotal role in changing our perception about forgiving ourselves?

(Coach Read)

It says in John 2:2 that *"Jesus is the sacrifice that makes up for our sins and the sins of everyone else in the world".* If Christ's death on the cross can cover everyone's sins. Why can't you let go of your mistakes and bad choices from the past? Sin is usually viewed by people at different levels. Such as, you tell a little white lie and you reason in your heart that isn't as bad as telling lies all the time, right?

The truth is, all sin is sin in God's eyes (James 2:10). You either sin or don't (We all sin). Sin is what keeps us from being close to God. Christ is the link between God and us, God sent Christ to you because He wants you and loves you very much.

Once we are in Christ, sin no longer has power over us. God says in *Romans 8:1-2 "that there is no condemnation",* so why would we go against the Creator of the world by condemning ourselves? In other words, what we are saying when we do this, is that Jesus is not enough.

He is enough and we can take Him at His word, we are forgiven of all of our sins from yesterday, today, and tomorrow. Simply let go of your past sin towards someone, surrender it to God, and allow God's truth of forgiveness to be your new reality.

Q18. Why do we condemn ourselves when God offers forgiveness and says there is no condemnation in Him (Romans 8:1-2)?

(Student Read)

To live in the freedom of self-forgiveness it is vital to spend time with God renewing your mind and praying Romans 12:1-2. Renewing your mind with the Word of God is literally cleaning the lenses you view everything with. How you perceive God, the world around you, and yourself is influenced by what goes into your mind.

> God never said that forgiveness would be easy. In fact, sometimes the opposite is true, but take heart in God's word and accept His truth for your own life. His instructions to us really do work, they will lead us into pathways of righteousness where we can live again.

Over time we will begin to find ourselves free from the ghost of our past, we will walk with no more guilt, no more hiding, and no more shame. We will just be free in God's love.

"Therefore, having put away falsehood, let each one of you speak the truth with his neighbor, for we are members one of another. Be angry and do not sin; do not let the sun go down on your anger, and give no opportunity to the devil. Let the thief no longer steal, but rather let him labor, doing honest work with his own hands, so that he may have something to share with anyone in need.

Let no corrupting talk come out of your mouths, but only such as is good for building up, as fits the occasion, that it may give grace to those who hear. And do not grieve the Holy Spirit of God, by whom you were sealed for the day of redemption. Let all bitterness and wrath and anger and clamor and slander be put away from you, along with all malice.

Be kind to one another, tenderhearted, forgiving one another, as God in Christ forgave you." (Ephesians 4:25-35)

It is difficult to let go of resentment toward those who have wronged us. But that is precisely what God commands us to do—not only for their benefit but also for our own. Unforgiveness causes stress and unhappiness, which can pervade our interactions with coworkers, friends, and family. When we choose to forgive others and ourselves, however, we will find freedom.

Q19. What role does renewing your mind with the Word of God play in the process of self-forgiveness?

Q20. How does the word of God influence our perception of God, the world, and ourselves?

A GUY WHO FOUND FORGIVENESS

(Coach Read)

Thomas was known as the town 'curmudgeon', a man who held onto grudges tighter than a hoarder would hold his gold. The bitter seeds of the past had firmly rooted within him, each unforgiven act snaking its vines around his weary heart. He held grudges against friends and family and worst of all, he had a hard time forgiving himself for the mistakes he had made.

Life had not been particularly kind to Thomas - he had experienced numerous betrayals, financial losses, and personal failures. He held onto these bitter memories, replaying them over and over like a broken track, which only fueled his inability to forgive. His personal relationships suffered, he distanced himself from his friends, and his family hesitated to engage with him. Inwardly, something gnawed at him-- a longing for peace he couldn't ignore anymore.

One day, Thomas met the town's Pastor Harper, and unburdened himself, revealing his inability to forgive others and himself. Harper listened with compassion and then said,

> "Thomas, you must find the courage to let go of the bitterness that plagues you. You should consider surrendering your burdens to God. Unshackle yourself from the chains of the past and embrace His forgiveness."

Skeptically, but desperate for peace, Thomas began to regularly attend the church. He spent quiet moments in prayer, confessing his resentment and his inability to forgive. He read Romans 12:1-2, which talked about renewing your mind and how it could transform one's life. He learned about forgiveness as it was interpreted in Ephesians 4:25-35. The idea of setting aside all falsehood and embracing truth, letting go of anger, and treading on a path of kindness profoundly resonated with him.

As he read the Bible and contemplated its teachings, he started noticing a change within himself. The Word of God was like an ointment on his wound, it began to clean the lens with which he saw the world and himself, softening the hardened edges of his heart. As he daily read his Bible, attended more sermons, and engaged in more prayer, he slowly started unpacking the grief and bitterness that had entwined his soul.

Thomas began to grasp the idea of forgiveness, not just as an act of kindness towards others but as a means for his own spiritual liberation. It wasn't an easy path, but each verse committed to memory, each prayer whispered in the stillness of the church, seemed to lighten his burden.

> He finally found himself at a point where he could let go of his resentment toward those who had wronged him. The act of forgiving opened a floodgate of relief within him. The unexpected outcome was his ability to forgive himself, to see his past mistakes not as burdens, but as lessons that had shaped his life. The ghost of his past no longer walked with him, his guilt started fading, and with it, his shame.
>
> The transformative power of God's love left Thomas a changed man. He found himself able to interact with those around him without bitterness tainting his every word. He walked with lighter steps, held his head up higher, and he was free in God's love.

Thomas' story stands as a testament to the healing power of forgiveness, the essence of which lies in the pages of the Bible, in our ability to surrender our burdens to God, and in the quiet willingness to accept His love and truth for our lives.

Q21. What steps did Thomas take to overcome his inability to forgive others and himself?

Q21A. And what changes did he experience as a result?

Q22. After going through this Key, do you feel that forgiveness is important to being set free?

Q22A. What are the next steps that you will take to forgive yourself and others?

Pray: First let God know you accept full responsibility for your unforgiving attitude, then admit the truth, let God know you have battled with unforgiveness and desire to be set free from it. Lastly, pray for the persons who have wronged you.

KEY 8: WHAT I SAY MATTERS

Take a moment before you begin to discuss Key 7 Forgiveness. Share with each other how God led you to take the next steps in order to be set free.

(Coach Read)

Let no foul language escape your lips, but if something is good for the edification of a need, (let it leave your lips) so as to give grace to those who hear. I recall my mother rinsing my mouth out with soap when I was a child. She escorted me to the kitchen sink, rubbed a bar of soap in my mouth, rinsed it out with water, and then made me return to my room.

I got in trouble because I repeated a curse phrase I heard a friend use, and my mother overheard me say it. That day, I learned my lesson and resolved to never use that word again.

Our words are a spiritual gauge that shows how much of our soul we have surrendered to God. If we have allowed the Word of God to renew our minds, our conversation will undoubtedly reflect what we have learned. If we have not been engrossed by God's word, our old habits of speech and beliefs will betray us and reveal our true spiritual condition.

When my soul was not in harmony with God, I could tell because the words that came out of my mouth were carnal in nature.

> *"For those who live according to the flesh set their minds on the things of the flesh, but those who live according to the Spirit set their minds on the things of the Spirit. For to be carnally minded is death, but to be spiritually minded is life and peace." (Romans 8:5-6)*

When my speech lacked the fruit of the Spirit, I realized I had more flesh in me than the Spirit. What naturally comes out of my mouth is always a reflection of where my heart is.

As a Christian, having a carnal mindset means having a mindset that is focused solely on the desires of the flesh, disregarding spiritual values and principles. It is important to note that as humans, we are all susceptible to having a carnal mindset, but as Christians, we are called to resist it.

Q1. How can our speech patterns act as an indicator of our spiritual condition?

Q2. How does the Christian notion of resisting a carnal mindset align with the values and principles we should strive to uphold?

THE POWER TO SPEAK WORDS OF LIFE STARTS IN THE HEART

(Student Read)

Why should my mother wash my mouth out with soap, because I said a bad word that a friend taught me? She did it because she believed Jesus when he said, *"It is not what goes into a man's mouth that defiles him, but what comes out of his mouth". (Matthew 15:11)*

So, my mother was telling me that I had made myself dirty by saying the bad word, and she wanted me to understand that what I say matters. But, really, what's the big deal about saying a curse word? It didn't really hurt anyone. It's not like you were using the Lord's name in vain. Why are you getting so worked up about it? What's so bad about saying a curse word?

The answer is that when I said the bad word, I meant it negatively. What I said was devoid of affection, goodwill, and kindness. There was no moral radiance, holiness, or love. If it is not beautiful and uplifting then I should not say it at all.

In Ephesians 4:29, Paul describes it as a "rotten word," or an unclean word. He basically stated that it came from the garbage heap of pride.

The context is that bad words should not come out of our mouths as something normal.

> *"The good person out of the good treasure of his heart produces good, and the evil person out of his evil treasure produces evil, for out of the abundance of the heart his mouth speaks." (Luke 6:45)*

In Mathew 12:34-35 Jesus was talking to the Pharisees and said to them "You brood of vipers! How can you speak good, when you are evil? For out of the abundance of the heart the mouth speaks. The good person out of his good treasure brings forth good, and the evil person out of his evil treasure brings forth evil."

Q3. How does the use of "bad words" reflect the condition of one's heart?

Q4. Why is it considered wrong to use offensive language or curse words according to the Bible?

(Coach Read)

Jesus warns us that a life consumed by worldly cares and treasures will result in fruitless talk that will bring us judgment. A life surrendered to God and filled with the Holy Spirit results in speech that is full of God's grace, mercy, love, and power. I thank God that my mother was an intensely moral person who was passionately Christian.

She knew that soap in the mouth couldn't touch the dirt in my heart. If she had thought it could, she would not have been saddened by my choice of action.

"We must throw aside our old, arrogant selves because it is corrupt with selfish desires. And put on the new, gentle self that God himself fashioned in his own image through righteousness and holiness". (Ephesians 4:22–24)

In other words, you need a profound renewal of the mind and spirit. The struggle for purity in the lips ultimately takes place in the heart because the mouth speaks from the wealth of the heart.

Q5. What worldly cares and treasures do you currently wrestle with and how do you see it affect what you say?

(Student Read)

What we say and how we say it matters a lot. We are either used by Satan to destroy God's kingdom or by the Holy Spirit to build up God's Kingdom.

Every time we open our mouths to speak, we advance either the kingdom of life or the kingdom of death. No matter where we are on the planet, we can be filled with the Holy Spirit and have Him as our personal guide through life.

"But when He, the Spirit of truth, comes, He will guide you into all the truth; for He will not speak on His own initiative, but whatever He hears, He will speak; and He will reveal to you what is to come," Jesus said in John 16:13.

In other words, God will reveal to us all the guidance we will need, including what to say, through the Holy Spirit.

Q6. How does our speech reflect either the advancement of God's Kingdom or the destruction of it?

Q7. How does the verse from John 16:13 support the idea of divine guidance in our choice of words through the Holy Spirit?

SPEAK WORDS OF LIFE

(Coach Read)

Satan tempted Eve in the Garden of Eden by speaking to her. Eve didn't realize it, but when she and Adam discussed Satan's idea, she advanced the kingdom of death through her spoken words.

God said, *"Because you have listened to the voice of your wife, and have eaten from the tree about which I commanded you, saying, you shall not eat from it; cursed is the ground because of you; in toil you will eat of it all the days of your life." (Genesis 3:17 NASB)*

Satan tricks us into believing his falsehoods, but it's only when we actually speak them into life that they bring the kingdom of death to us. When Satan lied to Adam and Eve, they did not capture their thoughts and surrender them to God. Instead, they believed the lie of Satan and discussed them as words of truth which became the reality for their lives.

"We demolish arguments and every pretension that sets itself up against the knowledge of God, and we take captive every thought to make it obedient to Christ." (2 Corinthians 10:5)

Do not allow the words of Satan to come out of your mouth, take those thoughts captive and give them to God, and never think about them again.

As *Proverbs 18:21 says "Death and life are in the power of the tongue, and those who love it will eat its fruit"*. Words are incredibly powerful. Believe it or not, words can build up, bless, curse, encourage, and motivate or they can also tear down, hurt, and cause horrible scars.

A soothing tongue [speaking words that build up and encourage] is a "Tree of Life", but a perversive tongue [speaking words that overwhelm and depress] crushes the spirit (Proverbs 15:4).

Make your mouth a fountain of life and not death. Be slow to speak and swift to hear. Seek opportunities to speak kind, tenderhearted words that build up and not tear down; encourage more and criticize less.

"Let no unwholesome word proceed out of your mouth, but only that which is good for building up, that it may give grace to the listeners". (Ephesians 4:29)

Q8. How can someone use their words to positively impact others rather than causing harm or discouragement?

(Student Read)

The Holy Spirit will only share with you the words that can bring life to you.

For example, I love you, you're such a blessing, you look great, I see you doing great things, you are smart, you're so thoughtful, you can do all things in Christ, I forgive you, I'm committed to you, life is better because of you. We could go on and on, but the point is to avoid saying anything unwholesome. Capture them before they escape your mouth.

> It's only fair to give you examples of words of death. They are:
>
> I hate you; I wish you had never been born, you're ugly, you'll never amount to anything, you're stupid, you're selfish, you shouldn't even try, you're a failure, I never want to see you again, I want a divorce, you were a mistake, it's all about your fault and so on.

Again, we could go on and on about words of death until you realize that saying them will never bring you life. They will only bring you misery and suffering.

When someone says, through words or actions, "I feel worthless," "I can't do anything right" "I don't know why God made me," "No one cares," or "I hate my life," we have an opportunity to speak life into that person. We can follow the example of our Savior and proclaim good news to the poor, liberty to captives, recovery of sight to the blind, and freedom to the oppressed (Luke 4:18). We can speak life and hope to this world.

If you are the person who is saying these things, reject being negative and pessimistic about everything. Don't allow yourself to speak words of doom with gloomy ramifications. Change course and begin seeing everything optimistically from Christ's perspective.

Q9. What is the difference between the words of life and the words of death highlighted in this passage?

Q10. How does the text suggest we should respond when confronted with someone expressing a negative point of view?

WE MUST GUARD OUR HEARTS

(Coach Read)

To keep our tongues from speaking Satan's lies, we will need God's help to become more like Him. We were created in the image of God to speak life-giving words that build up, heal, and encourage. In order for there to be transformation, we must first learn what can help us have success.

As we talked about earlier, we must guard our hearts. *"Whatever is in your heart determines what you say." (Matthew 12:34)* The words we speak reflect our inner state of mind. If we want to master our tongue, we must first master the junk that bombards our ears and saturates our souls.

We don't get into trouble because we are focused on Jesus all the time; we get into trouble because we are focused on things that have distracted us from knowing Him as our Savior.

Satan can use TV, music, talk shows, podcasts, friends, what we read, and anything else that is not in line with God's truth to confuse and deceive you. If we have to justify our actions in any way, it is a clear indication that we are speaking Satan's lies.

For example, many Christians believe it is acceptable to consume alcohol and justify it by claiming that they never get drunk. Granted, drinking wine or other alcoholic beverages is not a sin in and of itself; what is a sin is based on why you are drinking an alcoholic beverage.

Could you be drinking alcohol to numb some pain or weariness in your life? Do you have to drink alcohol with every meal, or can you go many meals without thinking about it? If you have to justify why you are drinking alcohol or anything else that can harm your body, you are speaking a lie of Satan into your life.

Be honest with yourself about the reasons behind your actions. Make sure that what you are doing is bringing glory to God. If it is, then feel free in your heart and mind and continue to speak life into your life. However, refrain from justifying the reasons behind your actions.

Q11. What is the significance of mastering our inner state of mind according to the passage?

Q12. How does it relate to justifying actions like consuming alcohol as a Christian?

(Student Read)

We cannot find consistent success in speaking words of life into our lives unless we protect our hearts from everything the world has to offer. I said the bad word because my friend said it, my friend was used by Satan to deceive me into thinking it was ok to say the bad word. Because I did not guard my heart, I followed his lead and spoke a word that ultimately could lead to death.

The same can be said about drinking alcohol or engaging in any other activity that has the potential to harm us or lead us down a dangerous path. The fact that everyone else is doing it or that we have convinced ourselves in our hearts that it is acceptable in spite of having addictive behavior is not okay. The true reasons behind our actions lie deep within us long before they are expressed in words.

> As God's children, we are constantly exposed to negative influences, but if my heart is determined not to believe the lies that the world offers me then I will then be able to triumph over the darkness that is constantly knocking on my door.

What happens when we guard our hearts, is we begin to hear the lies of the world as opportunities to speak the truth of God's word. Every time Satan attacks us with his lies, we respond with God's truth. Satan's voice weakens, while God's truth and His words of life strengthen us.

Words no longer can bring death to your life; you will begin to find freedom and no longer live with inconsistencies in what you say.

Q13. How does guarding our hearts help in resisting the negative influences of the world and speaking life-giving words?

(Coach Read)

The Bible says in *Colossians 3:8* that *"We must rid ourselves of all such things as anger, rage, malice, slander, and filthy language from our lips"*. If we are determined in our hearts to not allow words of death to control us, we must stop allowing Satan to lead us into destructive behavior.

Cry out loud to God when things are hard, and place yourself in a position that can help lead you to speak words of life into yourself. *"Take control of what I say O Lord and guard my lips"*. *(Psalms 141:3)* Determine in your heart that it is God's way or no way at all.

> *"That we are to keep our mouth shut and speak little" (Proverbs 10:19).*

Sometimes we just need to shut our mouths and refuse to speak unless we have life-giving words to say. Do the opposite of what you used to do when you spoke without thought or care. Instead of acting foolishly, only speak when God's word has given you peace and words of life flow.

Sometimes, saying nothing is the best thing to do. Jesus didn't say anything a lot of the time, even when He was treated very badly. Even though Jesus never did anything wrong, the Bible says that the things He went through taught him how to be obedient.

> *"When being reviled and insulted, He did not revile or insult in return." (1 Peter 2:23)*

> *(Proverbs 17:27-28) says "A truly wise person uses few words; a person with understanding is even-tempered. Even fools are thought wise when they keep silent; with their mouths shut, they seem intelligent".*

Q14. What lessons can we learn about controlling one's anger and the use of words?

SPEAKING WORDS OF LIFE, NOT GOSSIP.

(Student Read)

Gossip essentially involves discussing others in a negative manner, potentially influencing others to do the same. It is frequently intentional and aimed at harming someone's reputation or merely highlighting the flaws (or wrongdoing) of others.

Although one might assume that gossip is confined to dissatisfied employees in an office, it is present everywhere, including within Christian communities. Many times, we feel the urge to criticize fellow believers when we perceive their behavior as unchristian or in violation of biblical teachings.

However, we often overlook the fact that we ourselves were and still are sinners. It is important for us to avoid getting involved in gossip, whether it occurs among fellow believers or in society at large.

We should make an effort to stop it from spreading. Gossip has many negative effects on people. Innocent small talk between friends can escalate into a larger discussion that is overheard by others who were not initially involved.

Often, the things being talked about are more speculation without any evidence or substantiation. And even if there is evidence, what positive outcomes can result from engaging in such discussions?

As Christians, we should consistently use our words with the same intention of love that Jesus would have had. We must always refrain from using our words to cause harm or tear others down. Our words should always be employed to uplift others and inspire them.

Q15. What are some of the potential negative effects of engaging in gossip?

Q16. Why is it important for individuals, particularly within Christian communities, to resist the urge to partake in such discussions?

A LADY WHO HAD A BAD HABIT OF GOSSIPING

(Coach Read)

Suzy, a beautiful vibrant young lady had an unfortunately stinging bad habit - she loved to gossip. Her days were spent spinning tales about the lives of her neighbors, acquaintances, and even her own friends. Her words were hardly ever uplifting, more like a strong wind tearing down the carefully built houses of others' reputation.

Suzy owned a small café in the center of town, and it was there that the seeds of gossip took root and flourished abundantly. Despite the coffee being of the best quality, there was something a bit bitter about the café, a hollow echo in the laughter, a veiled darkness in the corners of otherwise lively conversations.

One Sunday afternoon, while washing the dishes after a long day at the café, Suzy noticed a gentle humming coming from her grandmother's old radio. She knew that voice – it was the local Pastor delivering his weekly sermon about the virtues of humility, kindness, and speaking well of one another.

As she listened to the sermon, Suzy felt a sudden jolt, as though being pricked by a thorn. The Pastor spoke of the sin of pride, and how it displays a false sense of superiority over others. He started explaining how gossip was a manifestation of pride, disguising itself as idle chatter. It spread the idea that one individual might be more righteous than the other when in truth, all are equal in the eyes of God.

> Suzy felt a chill run down her spine. At that moment, it was as if God was speaking directly to her, unmasking the truth of her gossiping habit. She realized the destructive nature of her words, how they broke down rather than built up, how they turned her into a judge rather than a gracious human being, positioning her as if she were higher and holier.

> With teary eyes and a heavy heart filled with newfound awareness, she whispered, "God, I repent for my sin." Suzy repented for her indiscretions, feeling a burden lifted off her heart. She yearned to seek forgiveness not only from God but from all those she'd wronged.

In the days that followed, Suzy took Godly counsel to heart. The café became a domain of cheer and upliftment. Her conversations were now filled with words of life that motivated and brought out the best in people. In this newfound attitude, Suzy found herself free from her old chains of pride and judgment. In its place was a warmth, a joy that radiated from being the source of elevating others rather than pulling them down.

It was not a simple journey, and temptation often knocked on her door, but with every passing day, Suzy chose compassion over condemnation, love over disdain, and understanding over prejudice.

In this transformation, the small-town café once associated with bittersweet feelings became the beating heart of the community - a place to share, to grow, and to celebrate the good in each other. Through God's wisdom, Suzy's repentance brought about a swell of kindness, reminding everyone that when we speak about others, it should be to elevate them above ourselves.

Q17. What sparked Suzy's realization about the destructive nature of her gossiping habit?

Q17A. And what change did it bring about in her and her café?

WORDS CAN CHARACTERIZE ENTIRE FAMILIES

(Student Read)

Someone told me when I was a kid that I was a loser and that my life would be meaningless. Those words changed the course of my life, and I was determined to prove them wrong. I made a decision in my life from that point forward to do whatever it took to achieve success, no matter who I had to hurt in the process.

The world system is set up to control and or dominate weaker people. When we are walking in the world system, we use our words to control or dominate those we feel are inferior to us. I hurt a lot of people with my words especially when I felt they were not on my side. Every person who is not walking in the Spirit has said things to others that are hurtful.

Certain hurtful words can sometimes characterize entire families. Words like, they're just a bunch of drunks, none of them finished school, they're lazy, dumb, angry people, whatever it is, you don't have to believe the lie any longer. I was told I was a loser and nobody told me that I didn't need to believe that. Only by God's grace and by believing God's truth about me, that I am now free from that lie.

According to *Exodus 20:5, "sin and its consequences can be passed down from generation to generation."* If your family has any kind of generational sin, the good news is that you can be free of it! You have the opportunity to be the first generation to walk in freedom, thereby beginning a chain reaction of God's loving kindness and blessing to a thousand generations after you (Exodus 20:6).

> Ask God to shine a light on words that should have never been spoken to you and denounce them now in Jesus' name! From this day on do not ever allow those lies into your mind or heart.

Q18. How did the use of hurtful words and the belief in a lie impact the personal journey described in this text?

Q19. How does the reference to Exodus 20:5 and 20:6 provide a means for overcoming generational sin and altering future generations?

(Coach Read)

Someone once wrote a declaration for their life and I believe they are God's words for us today. Say them aloud and believe them with all your heart.

I am blessed with God's supernatural wisdom, and I have a clear direction for my life.

I am blessed with creativity, courage, ability, and abundance.

I am blessed with a strong will, self-control, and self-discipline.

I am blessed with a great family of God who love me.

I am blessed with faith, God's favor, and fulfillment.

I am blessed with supernatural strength and divine protection.

I am blessed with an obedient heart that has a positive outlook on life.

I reject any curse that has ever been spoken over me, any negative evil word that has ever come against me, I believe is broken right now in Jesus' name.

I am blessed wherever I go.

Everything I put my hands to is going to prosper and succeed for God's glory.

I am blessed because I am God's child and He says so and I believe Him.

Pray: Humble yourself before the Lord, and speak to Him the life-giving words He has for you. Confess to Him those times you spoke death into your own and other people's lives. Repent and let God know your intention to only speak words of life from now on.

KEY 9: SATAN WANTS YOU BLIND, STUPID, AND MISERABLE

(Coach Read)

John Piper once said, that one of life's most sobering facts is that all humans have a supernatural adversary whose goal is to use pain and pleasure to make us blind, stupid, and miserable — forever. He is referred to in the Bible as *"the devil and Satan, the deceiver of the whole world... the accuser" (Revelation 12:9-10), "the ruler of this world" (John 12:31), and "the god of this age" (2 Corinthians 4:4).*

God is supreme over Satan. In this world, the devil does not have a free hand. He is restrained so that he can do no more than God allows. In effect, he must obtain permission, as Jesus reveals in the case of Simon Peter, *"Simon, Simon, behold, Satan has asked to have you, that he may sift you like wheat" (Luke 22:31). "Behold, Job is in your hand; only spare his life,"* the Lord said to Satan *(Job 2:6).*

So clearly, God sees Satan's ongoing role as essential to his purposes in the world, because if God so desired, Satan would be thrown into the lake of fire now, rather than at the end of the age. *"The devil who had deceived them was cast into the lake of fire and... will be tormented day and night for all eternity." (Revelation 20:10)* His total defeat is unavoidable. But not just yet.

In order to overcome Satan and prevent ourselves from succumbing to addictions or hang-ups, we must thoroughly understand his strategy. A quarterback for an American football team must not only know his team's offensive plays but also the defensive plays of his opponents. He will not be able to defeat the opponent if he does not properly prepare; the same is true for us when dealing with our advisor Satan. Our offensive weapon is the complete armor of God, which includes the word of God. We must utilize the word of God to conquer Satan whenever he attacks.

Q1. Based on the reference of an American football team, how does the text suggest we can understand and counteract Satan's strategies?

Q2. What is the role of God's word in this process?

A LADY THAT WAS DECEIVED BY SATAN

(Student Read)

Jessica, a devoted Christian, lived a peaceful life, attending church regularly, and praying fervently, but was oblivious to the subtle attacks that Satan had been orchestrating in her life.

Jessica had always been receptive to knowledge, she studied everything, always believing that knowledge was power. One day, Satan disguised his first strategy as wisdom, embedding lies in the perceived truth she eagerly sought. He slowly instilled in her mind doubts about the fundamental truths of Christianity. Intriguing philosophies and theories began to seem logical to Jessica, and she unknowingly hoarded these falsehoods in her heart.

This caused Jessica to question her faith for the first time in her life. The second strategy that later was revealed to Jessica, is because she began to question her faith Satan created unbelief in God and gradually, she stopped believing. The distortion had begun, and faith in God seemed to be more of a fairy tale, causing Jessica to question God's existence itself. She slowly distanced herself, her prayers growing shallow, her visits to the church less frequent.

Thirdly, cloaked in the very light and righteousness that defined her faith, Satan drew her deeper into deception. His masquerade as an angel of light caused her to see him as a reflection of God's glory, not as the manipulator he truly was. She began to see what was wrong as right and what was right as wrong.

In the fourth instance, he materialized his deceptive signs and wonders. Miracles and prophetic visions came to her that were so real, that Jessica started interpreting them as authentic signs from God, not recognizing the source of this deception. She started reading her horoscope every day and visited tarot card readings as her life gradually fell apart.

Satan's fifth move was to tempt her. Just like the Serpent in Eden, he lured her towards worldly pleasures, enticing her mind with the promise of contentment and joy outside of her Faith. The worldly allure grew stronger, pulling her gradually away from the path she once tread upon. She began experimenting with drugs and was enticed by a man to participate in orgy parties.

The sixth strategy involved the manipulation of God's word. He twisted the Scriptures, feeding her distorted interpretations that began to make sense in her doubting mind. She started to focus on parts of the Bible that seemed to justify her actions, completely overlooking the core truths and God's true commandments.

His seventh move was an assault on her health. Jessica, once filled with vibrancy and vitality, began to wither like a leaf in autumn. Unseen diseases and sickness besieged her, the strength and protection she would have sought from God, were now absent due to her drifting faith.

The eighth and final tactic was accusing her of her past failures. Memories of her past mistakes started to haunt her relentlessly. Shame and guilt, instead of forgiveness, were her constant companions. She felt condemned, unworthy of God's grace, and forgotten.

However, Jessica's struggle did not go unnoticed. Suzie, her small group leader recognized her diminishing faith and went to her house to talk. One day, she visited her and held her hand, praying over her. She quoted Psalms 46:1, "God is our refuge and strength, an ever-present help in trouble." She encouraged her to find strength in God's words and resist the devil's deception.

Gradually, Jessica with Suzie's help began to understand how she'd been lured by Satan's lies. Each deception was revealed, and she resolved to guard herself against them. Her faith was renewed, and she developed a deeper love for God. Armed with discernment and a true understanding of God's word, Jessica defied Satan's strategies, reclaiming her life, her health, and her relationship with God.

From that point onward, Jessica lived out the truth of *Ephesians 6:11, "Put on the full armor of God, so that you can take your stand against the devil's schemes".*

Q3. What strategies did Satan use to deceive and lead Jessica astray from her Christian faith?

Q4. How did she eventually overcome this deception to reclaim her relationship with God?

----

8 STRATEGIES SATAN USES TO DESTROY US

PLAYBOOK STRATEGY 1: HE DISGUISES LIES AS TRUTH

(Coach Read)

Our world is filled with con artists, liars, and thieves who seek to defraud us. But the Bible warns us about the greatest deceiver of all—Satan the Devil.

One method that Satan can wreak devastation in your life is by convincing you of a lie disguised as the truth. Because we are ignorant of God's truth, his lies can make us easy targets. *"When he lies, he speaks according to his own nature, for he is a liar and the father of lies," (John 8:44)* When Satan first makes his appearance in the Bible in Genesis 3, his opening statement, *"Did God declare, you must not eat of any tree in the garden?"* raises doubts about the veracity of the statement.

The second thing he said, "You won't die," was a subtly misleading statement. Because Satan lacks truth, according to John, "he has nothing to do with the truth" (John 8:44). All he does is lie to you.

> Do you think that because you are a religious person, you cannot be deceived? Jesus revealed that one of the most pervasive forms of deception is found in religious practice. And the Bible reveals who is behind many religious deceptions. Satan!

The Apostle Paul warns the Corinthians against false ministers: "For such are false apostles, deceitful workers, transforming themselves into apostles of Christ. And no wonder! For Satan himself transforms himself into an angel of light. Therefore, it is no great thing if his ministers also transform themselves into ministers of righteousness, whose end will be according to their works". (2 Corinthians 11:13–15)

Satan will use false teachers to promote his lies. These people may seem credible or authoritative and may use religious language or concepts to deceive people and promote falsehoods.

Yes, Satan has many strategies, schemes, and devices to deceive us. Some unknowingly worship him as an *"angel of light" (2 Corinthians 11:4)* while others look to him through séances, tarot cards, channeling, and astrology. Millions of people dabble in the occult and seek answers from soothsayers and mystics. These dark practices are deceptive, and most who call themselves Christians can recognize blatant Satanic influence.

As Christians, it is important to be discerning and test everything against the truth of God's word. We can guard against Satan's lies by studying the Bible, seeking God's guidance through prayer, and being open to correction and accountability from other believers.

Q5. What strategies does Satan employ to deceive people according to the passage?

Q5A. And how can Christians guard against these deceptions?

Q6. Can you think of a time Satan has lied and deceived you?

PLAYBOOK STRATEGY 2: HE CREATES UNBELIEF

(Student Read)

Satan will use circumstances and our unbelief to blind our minds from God's truth. *"The god of this age has blinded the minds of the unbelievers, to keep them from seeing the light of the gospel of the glory of Christ" (2 Corinthians 4:4).* So, he not only speaks what is false. He hides what is true. He keeps us from seeing the treasure of the gospel.

Satan's main goal is to prevent people from hearing the good news about Jesus. The message of forgiveness offered through Jesus Christ sets people free. As stated in an earlier key, *"So if the Son makes you free, you will be free indeed." (John 8:36)*

Another way Satan can cause us to have unbelief is to get us to deny that he exists. He seems to be most effective when people do not believe there is such a creature as the Devil. That hell is not real and we will never have to go there. If he can get people to doubt his existence, then he can do much of his work without their knowing.

This unbelief in his existence works to Satan's advantage. When people are either un-informed or misinformed about the existence of the Devil, they become like the Sadducees in Jesus' day, who did not believe in angels or spirits. When someone rejects the idea of Satan's existence, they are an easy target for him to manipulate.

If you have ever questioned if Satan or God are real and or even questioned if God loves you, then you have fallen prey to Satan's attack of unbelief.

Q7. What strategies does Satan use to instill unbelief?

Q7A. And how does this unbelief work to his advantage?

Q8. Has there been a time in your life when unbelief in God caused you to question His love for you?

PLAYBOOK STRATEGY 3: HE DISGUISES HIMSELF IN LIGHT AND RIGHTEOUSNESS

(Coach Read)

Satan disguises himself in light and righteousness to confuse you about what is true and what is false. Paul says in *2 Corinthians 11:13-15* that some people are posing as apostles who are not. *"Even Satan disguises himself as an angel of light,"* he says. It is not surprising that his servants disguise themselves as servants of righteousness."

> In other words, Satan has servants who profess enough truth to join the church and teach what Paul refers to as *"doctrines of demons"* from within *(1 Timothy 4:1)*. They will be like *"wolves in sheep's clothing"*, according to Jesus (Matthew 7:15).

> According to *Acts 20:30*, they *"will not spare the flock, but will lure people away to destruction"*. Our love will be sucked into stupidity without God's gift of discernment (Philippians 1:9).

As followers of Christ, we must be wary of those who claim to know God but have a different agenda that leads people away from total surrender to Jesus. The Holy Spirit is given to us by God to help us have discernment of these people, and we should not allow them to speak into our lives.

Many Christians have been harmed by these false believers and have strayed from their faith in Christ as a consequence. This is a significant tactic employed by Satan, which we must recognize to overcome him. Ensure that you are part of a Bible-believing Church, where the Pastor teaches the whole counsel of God in context. Surround yourself with individuals who wholeheartedly love Jesus and motivate you to seek Him every day.

Otherwise, you may become susceptible to Satan's deceptions and the falsehood that you might see on television or in written materials.

Q9. How does Satan use deception and false teachings within the church to lead people astray?

Q10. What advice is provided in the text to help believers discern and protect themselves from such tactics?

PLAYBOOK STRATEGY 4: HE DECEIVES BY SIGNS AND WONDERS

(Student Read)

Another strategy Satan employs against people is the use of signs and wonders to convince people that he is powerful. The last days are described in *2 Thessalonians 2:9, "The coming of the lawless one by the activity of Satan will be with all power, and with signs and wonders of the lie."* Some say it means "with false signs and wonders."

However, this makes the signs and wonders appear unreal. Some people believe that Satan can only perform bogus miracles. One thing is for certain his forgery will be convincing enough to fool almost everyone.

"God intends for a life of warfare with hell to be part of our preparation for heaven." One reason Satan can only fake his miracles is that Jesus describes the end times in Matthew 24:24 as follows: *"False Christs and false prophets will arise and show great signs and wonders, so as to lead astray, if possible, even the elect."*

Allow your faith to be founded on something far more profound than Satan's alleged inability to perform signs and wonders. Even genuine signs and wonders in support of anti-Christian claims prove nothing, even when performed in the name of Jesus. *"Lord, Lord, have we not done many great things in your name?" "I never knew you; depart from me, you workers of lawlessness,"* Jesus will respond (Matthew 7:22–23).

The issue wasn't that the signs and wonders weren't real, but that they were used to justify sin.

Q11. How does Satan use signs and wonders to deceive people?

Q12. Why should followers of Christ not base their faith solely on signs and wonders, even if they appear genuine?

PLAYBOOK STRATEGY 5: HE USES TEMPTATION TO DECEIVE YOU

(Coach Read)

(James 1:13) says when you are being tempted, do not say, *"God is tempting me."* God is never tempted to do wrong, and he never tempts anyone else. The only person that will attempt you to sin is Satan. He tried unsuccessfully to persuade Jesus to abandon the path of suffering and obedience in the wilderness (Matthew 4:1–11).

> In 2 Corinthians 11:3, Paul warns all believers against this: *"I am afraid that, as the serpent deceived Eve through his cunning, your thoughts will be led astray from a sincere and pure devotion to Christ."*

When difficult circumstances arise, we are tempted to seek relief from the pain we are experiencing. In the wilderness, Jesus was in pain, and Satan tempted him not to endure and trust God. If we are not aware that Satan wants to tempt us when we are at our weakest, we have a slim chance of overcoming the temptation. But know that God will always provide a way out of the temptation.

"No temptation has overtaken you except what is common to mankind. And God is faithful; he will not let you be tempted beyond what you can bear". (1 Corinthians 10:13) But when you are tempted, he will also provide a way out so that you can endure it.

As mentioned, multiple times before, when you feel tempted, say "No" out loud in the name of Jesus and move away from the situation. Do not remain engaged in what you are doing; Instead, change your location and surroundings. Take whatever actions necessary to remove yourself from your current situation. Above all, replace it with something that will honor and glorify God.

Q13. What role does Satan play in tempting individuals?

Q14. How can he use difficult circumstances to misguide people?

Q15. What strategies can individuals use to resist these temptations?

PLAYBOOK STRATEGY 6: HE LIES ABOUT GOD'S WORD

(Student Read)

If Satan can persuade you that God's word does not contain the answers you seek, he will suffocate your faith in God. In Mark 4:1-9, Jesus told the parable of the four soils. The seed of God's word is sown in it, and some of it falls on the path, where birds quickly take it away.

In verse 15, he explains, *"Satan immediately comes and takes away the word that was sown in them."* Satan seizes the word because he despises the faith that the word produces (Romans 10:17).

Paul expresses his concern for the faith in Thessalonians like this: *"I sent to learn about your faith, for fear that somehow the tempter had tempted you and our labor would be in vain" (1 Thessalonians 3:5).* Paul knew that Satan's design is to choke off the faith of people who have heard the word of God.

We must guard against doubt, by taking every negative thought captive and immediately surrendering it to God (2 Corinthians 10:5). Don't ever allow Satan to make you believe that God's word is not true. He is a liar and God and His word is truth (John 14:6)

Q16. What is the significance of the parable of the four soils?

Q17. How does it connect to the idea of Satan attempting to suffocate one's faith in God?

Q18. How can you make sure your faith in God doesn't grow weak?

PLAYBOOK STRATEGY 7: SATAN INFLICTS SICKNESS AND DISEASE

(Coach Read)

Another strategy Satan employs against us is to inflict sickness and disease on us. Jesus once healed a woman who was bent over and unable to straighten herself. When he was chastised for doing so on the Sabbath, he responded, *"Ought not this woman, a daughter of Abraham, whom Satan bound for eighteen years, be released from this bond on the Sabbath day?" (Luke 13:16)*

> **Notice that Jesus saw Satan as the source of the disease.**

God is sovereign over Satan. In this world, the devil has no free hand. He's on a leash and can only do what God allows. Peter described Jesus in *(Acts 10:38)* as someone who *"went about doing good and healing all who were oppressed by the devil."*

> **In other words, the devil frequently oppresses people who are afflicted.**

But don't fall into the trap of believing that every illness is the work of the devil. To be sure, while a "thorn in the flesh" may be God's design for our sanctification, it may also be a *"messenger of Satan" (2 Corinthians 12:7)*.

However, in other cases, the disease is attributed solely to God's design, with no mention of Satan: *"It was not that this man or his parents sinned, but that the works of God might be displayed in him". (John 9:3)* Jesus sees no reason to blame Satan for his own merciful intentions.

In some instances, sickness can be a result of sin in our own life. While sickness is not sin, the possibility of sickness can be the result of sin. Paul emphasized that our body is the temple of the Holy Spirit. He wrote the following to the Corinthians:

> *"Or do you not know that your body is a temple of the Holy Spirit within you, which you have from God, and that you are not your own? For you were bought with a price; therefore, glorify God in your body." (1 Corinthian 6:19, 20 NRSV)*

If you do have sickness the Bible tells us in *James 5:14. "Is anyone among you sick? Let them call the elders of the church to pray over them and anoint them with oil in the name of the Lord."* Make sure that if you are going with a broken and contrite heart, repent of any sin that you are aware of and be humble in the presence of God. Plead for mercy and allow God's grace to be manifested as He sees fit.

Q19. What are the different perspectives mentioned in the paragraph regarding the origins of sickness?

Q20. What solutions does the text suggest for those who are suffering from illness?

PLAYBOOK STRATEGY 8: HE ACCUSES US OF OUR PAST AND PRESENT SINS.

(Student Read)

Satan is constantly looking for ways to accuse you of your past and present actions. He will constantly remind you of your shortcomings and how God could never love you. *"Now the salvation and the power and the kingdom of our God and the authority of His Christ have come,"* says Revelation 12:10, *"for the accuser of our brothers has been thrown down, who accuses them day and night before our God."*

Satan's defeat is certain. But his accusations against you continue and this is one strategy he uses over and over again.

Religion teaches that in order for God to love you, you must do things in the form of works to please God. When you fail to be perfect, Satan is the first to remind you that you are flawed. He wants you to flee from God and believe the lies that you are unworthy.

> The truth is that you are not, and according to the Bible, we all fall short of God's glory (Romans 3:23). But now that we have been saved by grace through faith in Christ, we are no longer subject to our own perfection, but to His, Jesus sees us as His chosen people, not as sinners.

"We are now perfect saints, royal priests, a holy nation, and God's very own possession". *(Ephesians 2:8-9)* Satan will always try to get into your head and convince you that there is no hope for you. However, Jesus will always tell you that He loves you and will never condemn you (Romans 8:1).

Q21. What does the Bible say about Satan's accusations?

Q22. How does the concept of salvation by grace through faith in Christ shift our understanding of perfection and worthiness?

(Coach Read)

As a follower of Christ, we must always remember that the one who is in us is greater than the one who is in the world. (John 4:4) Never let Satan convince you that God does not love you and is angry with you. When we fall short, simply humble ourselves and run to Him, Satan uses this strategy to convince us not to run to Jesus.

Jesus will only love you and restore your faith, there is no lie in Him. This will take some time to get used to, you will have to keep telling yourself out loud, that God is not mad at you, He loves you regardless of the sin you have committed.

Remember that there are consequences for our actions and Satan will always exploit those to His benefit. However, God is capable of bringing all things together for the good of those who are called according to His purposes. We must acknowledge our wrongdoing and consequently distance ourselves from it, and repent ASAP. *(Romans 8:28) God is unable to associate with sin (1 John 1:7), but He will never abandon or forsake you (Hebrews 13:5).* His love for you is complete and final, nothing can ever change that.

> *"What, then, shall we say in response to these things? If God is for us, who can be against us? He who did not spare his own Son, but gave him up for us all—how will he not also, along with him, graciously give us all things?"*
>
> *Who will bring any charge against those whom God has chosen? It is God who justifies. Who then is the one who condemns? No one. Christ Jesus who died—more than that, who was raised to life—is at the right hand of God and is also interceding for us. Who shall separate us from the love of Christ? Shall trouble or hardship or persecution or famine or nakedness or danger or sword?*
>
> *As it is written: "For your sake, we face death all day long; we are considered as sheep to be slaughtered." No, in all these things we are more than conquerors through him who loved us.*
>
> *For I am convinced that neither death nor life, neither angels nor demons, neither the present nor the future, nor any powers, neither height nor depth nor anything else in all creation, will be able to separate us from the love of God that is in Christ Jesus our Lord. (Romans 8:31-39)*

If Satan is attacking you, it indicates that you are a child of God. Knowing his strategy is the first step in preventing him from deceiving you. Know the strategies he employs against you, be vigilant, and be determined in your heart to never fall for his lies.

Reject his lies with the Word of God and always run to Jesus; capture your negative thoughts and meditate on the truth. It is possible to break bad habits, but you must be familiar with the playbooks of Jesus and Satan.

Q23. What strategies does the passage suggest to handle the lies and deceiving tactics of Satan for followers of Christ?

Q24. What does it say about God's response when His followers fall short?

> **Pray:** Ask God to help you recognize Satan's attacks on your life as they occur. Request that He teaches you how to run to Him when you're most vulnerable and the temptations to sin are strong.

KEY 10: LIFESTYLE OF WORSHIP

(Coach Read)

What is worship? In the Merriam dictionary, Worship has been defined as an act of religious devotion usually directed towards a deity. It may involve one or more activities such as reverence, adoration, praise, and praying.

For many, worship is not about an emotion, it is more about a recognition of God and in some religions' gods. An act of worship may be performed individually, in an informal or formal group setting.

Worship, to a Christian, is an act of total surrender to Yahweh, the creator of the world.

We devote our entire lives to God's service; our lifestyle, likes, dislikes, interests, hobbies, and work are all coordinated with God's leadership and guidance.

We exist to declare Christ to the world and to work in unison with the Father, Son, and Holy Spirit. (John 17:21-23) "For me to live is Christ, and to die is gain," Paul said in Philippians 1:21.

Paul also told us in Galatians 2:20 "That we must crucify our old habits and stop living for ourselves. We now live by faith in God's Son, because Christ now dwells within us".

Someone once said that there are four types of worshipers:

Ankle deep worshipers

Knee deep worshipers

Waist deep worshipers

Center of the river worshipers.

Most people want to encounter God in ankle, knee, or even waist-deep water while remaining in control. In other words, many people want to do the right thing for God, but with just enough control that God doesn't push them too far.

Those who live this way have bought into the lie that if they surrendered to His authority, He would force them to do things they don't want to do. God will never call you to something for which He has not already prepared you; He will always work in your life in accordance with the gifts He has given you.

What Level of Worshiper Are You?

(Student Read)

Ankle-Deep Worshiper:

Although God's presence can be refreshing at times, we still have complete control over our lives. We can splash around in the shallow part and have fun before deciding to exit the river without allowing God to have any lasting impact on our lives.

Knee-Deep Worshiper:

We go out a little deeper and now we can sense God's current (His Presence), but we are still in charge. Knee-deep water allows us to see those who have gone into deeper waters and we can witness for ourselves that there is "fullness of joy" (Psalm 16:11) in His Presence, but we still feel safe on the riverbank.

Waist-Deep Worshiper:

His spirit is strongly flowing in this place. Although we have moved into deeper water, we still battle the current and work to maintain our touch with the bottom. We are frequently tempted to return to the riverbank out of fear, a fear of what other people will think, or fear of losing control. At this point, we make a significant choice. who will hold the reins of my life. God or I?

Middle of the River worshiper:

We can encounter God's presence in all of its richness here. We give up trying to be in charge and instead lift our feet and float, letting His current take us. We follow in His footsteps, see the world through His eyes, are joyful amid adversity, and are satisfied with life.

Q1. What differences are outlined in the progression from an Ankle-Deep Worshiper to a Middle of the River Worshiper?

Q2. How do each of these stages reflect the level of control an individual allows God to have in their life?

Q3. Which level of worshiper do you see yourself at currently?

(Coach Read)

In the first key, I discussed my garage experience, which helped reshape my life. That day, I felt a supernatural presence of God that the world was never able to give me. It had such an effect on my life that it caused changes in my character and personality.

I used to wake up angry and depressed, but now I look forward to starting my day by praising God for how wonderful He is. Everything transformed, and over time I began to think about how I can advance God's kingdom one disciple at a time. My daily act of worship to God was to position myself to speak life into everyone around me, but none of this came easily to me.

> Worshiping God as a way of living requires discipline and a lot of effort. Like any athlete that is wanting to achieve the highest level of success in their sport, they have to be disciplined. In *1 Corinthians 9:27, Paul stated, "He disciplines his body like an athlete, training it to do what it should."* He was afraid that if he preached to others, he would be disqualified if he didn't.

An athlete devotes a lot of time and effort to his talent and does everything possible to help his body perform at its best. He takes his activity seriously and does not allow himself to slack or be lazy.

The reverse can also be true; let's face it, having hang-ups and addictions requires a significant amount of effort. We put in a lot of effort in sports to be the best, and we do the same with our hang-ups; we are consistent in our bad habits and find methods to always get our fix so that our bodies are free of whatever is bothering us.

It requires discipline and dedication to constantly put ourselves in situations that are not in our best interests. After a while, we begin to do our hang-ups without thinking about it; it becomes a normal way of life. It now has control over us and determines the paths we will take in life.

As mentioned before, worship encompasses every aspect of our lives as we surrender to God. However, one crucial aspect of worship is singing praises to God. This becomes particularly important when faced with strong temptations or overwhelming life circumstances. When you find yourself in such situations, take time to go to a quiet place and play some praise and worship music.

Allow your soul to be refreshed as you listen to and sing along with the words being sung. Make it a habit to prioritize this above anything else in your life, replacing any negative habits with worship.

Q4. How did the author's garage experience and subsequent sense of a divine presence shape their life and character?

Q5. How does this experience compare to the discipline required by an athlete or an individual with a hang-up or addiction?

Q6. How can singing praise and worship help get you through tough times?

(Student Read)

When we choose God's love and make the decision in our hearts to surrender completely to Him, we start to understand that God is the most amazing thing that has ever happened to us. We begin to believe God when we embrace His love for us, and as our relationship with Him grows, we develop a deep affection for Him.

> Our affection for God transforms religious duties into relational delights and now like many martyrs of our faith, we will die for Him. What was once regarded as a responsibility has now become a personal devotion at all cost. It brings us tremendous joy to get to know Him personally and to follow and obey everything He thinks is best for our lives.
>
> We begin to comprehend what it means to sacrifice our desires for what God desires, and our lives become more fulfilling than they have ever been.

The Bible states in *(Psalms 37:4)*, *"Find delight in the Lord, and He will fulfill your heart' desires."* Satan may attempt to distort the meaning of this verse and lead you to believe it includes any desire you may have. However, the true context of this verse implies that when you find delight in the Lord, your desires will align with His own desires, and your heart will be in harmony with His.

What are God's desires? It is for us to fulfill the great commandment and great commission. A true worshiper of God is actively involved in God's plan for this world. He wants us to love Him with all of our heart, mind, and soul, and to love our neighbor as ourselves. Additionally, He wants us to make disciples in our local community, region, and beyond.

As mentioned in the introduction to this curriculum, I hope that you are actively involved in guiding someone through the process of "Keys to Being Set Free". By doing so, it is an act of worship, and God is glorified through your efforts. Be fruitful and multiply!

Q7. What does it mean to truly delight in the Lord?

Q8. How does this affect our personal desires and the fulfillment of God's desires and plan for the world?

(Coach Read)

The first idea of worship is introduced in *Genesis chapter 22, verses 1-10*. Abraham led a worshipful life. He worshiped God with fear, obedience, and a heart ready to give up everything for the glory of God. Let us read and unpack these verses about sacrifice.

> *"Sometime later God tested Abraham. He said to him, Abraham! Here I am, he replied. Then God said, take your son, your only son, whom you love—Isaac—and go to the region of Moriah.*

> *Sacrifice him there as a burnt offering on a mountain I will show you. Early the next morning Abraham got up and loaded his donkey. He took with him two of his servants and his son Isaac. When he had cut enough wood for the burnt offering, he set out for the place God had told him about.*

> *On the third day, Abraham looked up and saw the place in the distance. He said to his servants, stay here with the donkey while I and the boy go over there. We will worship and then we will come back to you.*

> *Abraham took the wood for the burnt offering and placed it on his son Isaac, and he himself carried the fire and the knife. As the two of them went on together, Isaac spoke up and said to his father Abraham, Father? Yes, my son?*

> *Abraham replied. The fire and wood are here, Isaac said, but where is the lamb for the burnt offering? Abraham answered God himself will provide the lamb for the burnt offering, my son. And the two of them went on together.*

> *When they reached the place God had told him about, Abraham built an altar there and arranged the wood on it. He bound his son Isaac and laid him on the altar, on top of the wood. Then he reached out his hand and took the knife to slay his son."*

Q9. Which key elements illustrate Abraham's devotion-filled life, characterized by reverence, obedience, and willingness to sacrifice everything for the honor of God?

(Student Read)

Abraham, like Adam and Eve in the Garden of Eden, was put to the test to demonstrate his devotion to God. Abraham was asked to do something that no parent should ever be asked to do: he was asked to sacrifice his son. I can imagine Abraham being confused, angry, and unsure if he even heard God properly.

What exactly do you want me to do? Are you certain, God? God, this makes no sense! Our real devotion to God, however, is revealed in those moments of uncertainty.

> Do we agree with Jesus when he says, "*Not my will, but your will be done?*" *(Luke 22:42).* Or do we say, "God, you're crazy, I'm not going to sacrifice my son," and then turn our backs on Him?

Because of the laws in place today, I doubt He would ever ask you to sacrifice your son, but He will ask you to sacrifice something in your life that is preventing you from knowing Him more deeply.

If there still is something controlling you, such as money, relationships, or material things, He will come to you by permitting circumstances to occur in your life that will force you to choose whether to follow Him or reject Him.

To truly worship God, you must commit to love Him and obey Him even when things are difficult in your life.

Q10. What does the story of Abraham's test indicate about the nature of devotion to God, particularly in moments of uncertainty or challenge?

Q11. What might God ask you to sacrifice in your life today, that is preventing you from knowing Him more deeply?

THE FULL ARMOR OF GOD

(Coach Read)

The best way to worship God is to get ready to be obedient. How can we worship God if we aren't ready for the fights that Satan and the world will throw at us? The best way to get ready is to put on every piece of God's armor every day, as Ephesians 6 says. The armor of God helps Christians fight against spiritual warfare that is real and always attacking.

Each piece of armor has a unique job and protects the wearer from temptation and the possibility of adding new hang-ups or addictions. By putting on all of God's armor, like an athlete does, we train ourselves to know God better and protect ourselves from Satan's attack.

The full armor of God helps us understand both God's playbook and Satan's playbook.

The armor of God is the Belt of Truth, the Breastplate of Righteousness, the Shoes of the Gospel of Peace, the Shield of Faith, the Helmet of Salvation, and the Sword of the Spirit (Word of God). Let us read Ephesians 6 and break down each component of the armor and how it can keep us from falling behind as God's worshipers.

> *"Finally, be strong in the Lord and in his mighty power. Put on the full armor of God, so that you can take your stand against the devil's schemes. For our struggle is not against flesh and blood, but against the rulers, against the authorities, against the powers of this dark world, and against the spiritual forces of evil in the heavenly realms.*
>
> *Therefore, put on the full armor of God, so that when the day of evil comes, you may be able to stand your ground, and after you have done everything, to stand. Stand firm then, with the belt of truth buckled around your waist, with the breastplate of righteousness in place, and with your feet fitted with the readiness that comes from the gospel of peace.*
>
> *In addition to all this, take up the shield of faith, with which you can extinguish all the flaming arrows of the evil one. Take the helmet of salvation and the sword of the Spirit, which is the word of God. And pray in the Spirit on all occasions with all kinds of prayers and requests. With this in mind, be alert and always keep on praying for all the Lord's people." (Ephesians 6:10-18)*

Q12. What are the components of God's armor as described in Ephesians 6?

Q13. How do they assist Christians in standing against spiritual warfare and deepening their understanding of God and Satan's strategies?

BELT OF TRUTH

(Student Read)

It can be difficult to put on God's protection on a daily basis if we have not made it our daily habit. *(Ephesians 6:14)* says *"Stand firm then, with the belt of truth buckled around your waist."*

Some translations use a phrase like: "having girded your loins with truth" The loin refers to the lower back but includes the crotch area. In ancient days, men would wear long robes that would get in the way of work or fighting, so they would wrap up the long, draping material. This was girding up their loin.

The Lord knew we needed truth to wrap our loins. No matter where we live or when we live, the Lord has seen all of our ways and how they have hurt us and taken us off track. He knows we need the truth.

The first thing the enemy often tries to shake in our lives is our sense of who we are. We need to know who we really are in Christ. And Jesus is the only one who can set us free in this way. We worship God by honoring Him, and by accepting the truth about ourselves, which is that our identity is found in Christ.

When we put on the belt of truth every day, we are essentially letting God know that we are firmly convinced and have found peace in our hearts with His word. We believe and accept His words as the ultimate truth.

Q14. What does the Belt of Truth, as mentioned in Ephesians 6:14, symbolize?

Q15. How does daily wearing it help believers honor God, stand against the enemy's tactics, and solidify their identity in Christ?

BREASTPLATE OF RIGHTEOUSNESS

(Coach Read)

Ephesians 6:14 says *"with the breastplate of righteousness in place"*. Righteousness means being made right. Sometimes Scripture refers to righteousness that Christ gives us, His righteousness (2 Corinthians 5:21).

Sometimes the Bible refers to righteousness as something that God does through us, such as *"the righteous acts of the saints." (Revelation 19:8)* Both types of righteousness protect the heart in everyday spiritual battles.

> We require not only Christ's complete righteousness but also the ongoing righteousness that comes as a result of God's gift.

The devil tempts us with various sinful entanglements, but righteousness guards our hearts (souls). God's directions are frequently regarded as burdens or killjoys. However, an act of worship by obeying God protects your spirit from being wounded by sin.

We demonstrate our worship of God daily by consciously deciding to lead a morally upright life. We need to prepare ourselves mentally and then embody the righteousness that God gives us through His Son.

Q16. What are the two types of righteousness mentioned in the Bible?

Q17. How do they protect one's heart in spiritual battles according to Ephesians 6:14?

GOSPEL OF PEACE

(Student Read)

(Ephesians 6:15) "and with your feet fitted with the readiness that comes from the gospel of peace." The Lord's very person and nature is one of peace. (Galatians 5:22)

The word "peace" implies "oneness" or "wholeness" in Greek. The gospel, which translates as "good news," is the forgiveness of sins as well as access to and oneness with God through trust in Christ.

This union with the Lord brings about a calm demeanor of peace.

Ephesians repeatedly reminds us to stay firm. Worrying is one of the simplest methods for the enemy to succeed in luring us away from our firm stand. We are robbed of peace when we bring anxiousness and worry with us.

> *"Be anxious for nothing, but in everything by prayer and supplication, with thanksgiving, let your requests be made known to God; and the peace of God, which surpasses all understanding, will guard your hearts and minds through Christ Jesus."*
>
> *(Philippians 4:6-7)*

But the gospel of peace maintains our feet firmly planted. We worship God by choosing to live in peace.

Q18. How does the concept of "peace" contribute to believers standing firm in their faith?

Q19. How does peace protect them from worry and anxiety?

SHIELD OF FAITH

(Coach Read)

Ephesians 6:16) "In addition to all this, take up the shield of faith" When Paul penned this passage, Roman soldiers carried heavy animal hide-covered shields. They would dip their shields into the water before a fight so that when fiery darts struck them, the wet hide would extinguish the darts.

Similarly, in order to be replenished and fully functional, a Christian's shield of faith must be routinely dipped in the water of God's word, because *"faith comes by hearing, and hearing by the word of God." (Romans 10:17)*

The shield of faith tells you to accept God's word as the ultimate authority and rest in it, while Satan will tell you to doubt it. We worship God by believing His word completely, we accept it in our hearts as absolute truth.

Q20. What is the significance of the 'shield of faith' according to Ephesians 6:16?

Q21. How is it connected to the practice of Christians immersing themselves in God's word?

THE HELMET OF SALVATION

(Student Read)

(Ephesians 6:17) "Take the helmet of salvation." Salvation occurs when we put our faith in Jesus' death, burial, and resurrection as payment for our sins. However, salvation is also accomplished through a long process of sanctification.

The helmet of salvation (like the breastplate of righteousness) is based on Christ's work to save us, but it also involves us as we journey with the Lord and enable Him to work salvation into every part of our minds.

The main spiritual battleground is the battlefield of our mind. While the enemy battles for strongholds to bind us, the Lord works His liberating truth into our perspectives.

We demonstrate our worship of God by taking control of our negative thoughts and by allowing God to guide and transform us according to His likeness. Allow God to have control over your life, step down from your position of authority, and trust in His guidance for your life. Find satisfaction and peace in His presence, and stop resisting Him any further.

Q22. What is the significance of the "helmet of salvation" in Ephesians 6:17?

Q23. How does it relate to the concept of sanctification and mental battles in the spiritual journey?

SWORD OF THE SPIRIT

(Coach Read)

(Ephesians 6:17) "and the sword of the Spirit, which is the word of God" The explanation of this piece of armor is right there in the verse, it is the "word of God".

Pastor Greg Laurie said it is the only piece of armor that is both defensive and offensive. When we are tempted, the most effective weapon that God has given to us as believers is the sword of the Spirit, which is the Word of God.

Jesus modeled this so beautifully during His temptation in the wilderness (Luke 4:1-13). When the devil tried temptation after temptation against Him, Jesus used the sword of the Spirit. When the devil tempted him three times, Jesus responded with the truth of God's word every time.

We worship God when we read God's word daily and use it to combat Satan's lies. Never be too busy to spend time in God's word daily. Make this a priority. You should never take a vacation from God's word. If this is not a priority in your life, everything else is vulnerable.

Q24. What example does Jesus provide that demonstrates the use of the "sword of the Spirit"?

\---

\---

Q25. Why is it important to make reading and using God's word a daily priority, according to Pastor Greg Laurie?

\---

\---

FINAL WORD ON WORSHIP

(Student Read)

Worship not only provides freedom in our own lives, but it also has the power to set others free. Paul and Silas are imprisoned in Acts 16:23-34. They were caught and beaten, and are now being held in a prison cell. What do they do, chained, tired, and surrounded by darkness, with every cause to be afraid?

They Worship! That night, many people found salvation, including the jailer and his complete family. That is the force of authentic worship. Chains are removed, and people are set free.

When God is the center of our love and attention, He will do far more than we can ask or imagine. (Ephesians 3:20) If you choose to adore Him with all of your heart, nothing will be impossible for you. Take your heart of worship to the world with the mindset to fulfill the "Great Commission" (Mathew 28:19).

You will see huge spiritual growth when you use this curriculum to teach other disciples. Together you will witness the decline of Satan's influence in people's lives and grow in God's grace, mercy, and love. It is possible to be set free through the power of Jesus. Do not underestimate the knowledge you have gained over these past months.

The most effective approach to maintaining one's freedom is to generously share the knowledge that has been given to you in this curriculum. Form a team of dedicated disciples who are (FAT) Faithful, Available, and Teachable who like you strive to disciple others. With the Holy Spirit's help, a powerful movement led by God can manifest as a result of your commitment to disciple others. Furthermore, as your disciples are guided by the Holy Spirit, they too can disciple others and a movement of God can happen in their ministry as well.

Before you know it, you can have thousands of disciples in your personal discipleship ministry. This was God's plan all along, each disciple having a personal ministry of disciples, discipling others.

Incorporate these teachings into your daily life, and gradually, you will see a transformation. Your old ways will pass away, and everything will become new. In Christ Jesus, victory is already assured. Remain steadfast and allow Him to fulfill His purpose in your life.

Please continue to have regular meetings with your coach and keep them informed about everything that God is accomplishing through your ministry. Make sure you are actively involved in a church that follows and believes in the teachings of the Bible. If you need assistance in finding a suitable church in your area or anywhere in the world, please reach out to your coach or contact Natural Discipleship, and someone will help you find a healthy Bible-believing church community.

Q26. How does the story of Paul and Silas demonstrate the transformative and liberating power of authentic worship?

Q27. How can this lesson contribute to fulfilling the "Great Commission" according to the text?

Q28. How important is it for you to have a personal discipleship ministry as an act of worship? Share your thoughts.

Pray: that God gives you a heart that wants to worship him in everything you do. Pray that every day he keeps making your heart clean and your eyes open to His truth.

CONGRATULATIONS

Congratulations on completing Natural Discipleship's "Keys to Being Set Free". We pray that God has opened your eyes to witness His magnificent presence in your life. We hope that He has initiated a process of change within you.

God works in various ways for each person, some experience instant transformation while others may progress at a slower pace. It is important to persistently seek Jesus daily and never lose hope. Remember that our ultimate destination is Heaven, so this life should be perceived as a continuous journey.

Continue to learn to love God every day and see everything from His perspective, keep on keeping on. Jesus says in Mathew 6:33, "Seek first the Kingdom of God and ALL things will be added onto you." All means all, you can't get any more than all, that's God's promise to you, except that as reality for your life.

You keep giving your all, if you fail, get back up and continue to run to Jesus, don't allow Satan to keep you in darkness. "Greater is He that is in you than he that is in this world" (1 John 4:4) You are a warrior in Christ created by God with a purpose to advance God's kingdom and to annihilate Satan and his lies. "You can do all things through Christ who strengthens you." (Philippians 4:13) Believe this and live it out loud every day of your life.

Could you please share your journey with us? We are a global community that has all struggled with hang-ups and addictions, and your story of transformation could give hope to many.

www.naturaldiscipleship.com/transform

Natural Discipleship, 10524 Moss Park Rd #204-339 Orlando Fl, 32832

info@naturaldiscipleship.com

COACH LEADERSHIP TRAINING GUIDE

GETTING STARTED WITH KEYS TO BEING SET FREE

Becoming a coach is a crucial next step in one's own journey toward being set free, and it is not just volunteer work, it's a calling. Coaching strengthens and supports one's own path to freedom. Acting as a coach for someone going through transformation reduces the likelihood of falling back into old habits. Mutual accountability is essential for the process of transformation and maintaining freedom from worldly bonds.

Now that you are currently going through "Keys to Being Set Free" or have completed all 10 Keys you are now encouraged to become a coach and teach what you have learned to others. As 1 Timothy 4:11-15 says, we should teach what we have learned. *"Don't let anyone look down on you because you are young, but set an example for the believers in speech, in conduct, in love, in faith and in purity. Until I come, devote yourself to the public reading of Scripture, to preaching and to teaching. Do not neglect your gift, be diligent in these matters; give yourself wholly to them, so that everyone may see your progress."*

Let's face it, we live in a damaged world, we all cope with the pains, hardships, and routines of daily life. We believe that no one is capable of or should seek to confront their hang-ups and pains on their own, that's where you come in as a coach. The key to each coach's success is determined by the humility of the coach. Never allow Satan to deceive you, convincing you that you are superior to others or that you have all the answers. Each time you enter a meeting with your student, you should do so with reverence for God, combined with humility and a sense of awe towards Him. You are on the same level as your student and your purpose is to help elevate them higher than yourself.

To coach someone is not an IQ test where only the intelligent can coach others. It is a community of strugglers looking to mend our brokenness, where IQ is irrelevant. In fact, if someone is too proud to go through the Keys to Being Set Free with you, then this curriculum is not intended for them. We should simply move on. We are a group of broken individuals in desperate need of a Savior, forming a supportive community where we bravely come together in a safe environment. We engage in this behavior because we desire a fervent, affectionate, and close relationship with Jesus. Moreover, we firmly believe that He is the sole solution for overcoming our hang-ups and dependencies throughout our lives.

We can't wait to hear all that God is going to do in your ministry, please keep us informed by sharing your stories with us at www.naturaldiscipleship.com/transfrom

CAN ANYONE BE A COACH?

The answer is yes if you are a person who is experiencing personal growth every day through the renewal of your mind through Christ Jesus (Romans 12:2). A coach is not a perfect individual but someone who acknowledges their brokenness with a contrite spirit (2 Corinthians 7:10). A coach is humble and seeks to draw closer to Jesus.

According to (Romans 6:14), sin does not have control over you because you are not under the law but under grace. Essentially, this verse implies that you are not trying to earn your way to heaven by being good enough, but rather seeking a closer relationship with God because you recognize your shortcomings and desperately need a Savior. We highly recommend that if you are a coach, you either are currently participating in the Natural Discipleship "Keys to Being Set Free" program or have completed the curriculum with your coach.

If you have not done so, we strongly encourage you to do it. If you require a coach to guide you through the program, please contact us at info@naturaldiscipleship.com, and someone will reach out to you.

WHAT IF I AM STILL ACTIVELY ENGAGED IN MY HANG-UP AND OR ADDICTION SHOULD I STILL COACH SOMEONE ELSE?

Shouldn't we share our experiences with others so they too can benefit from what we have learned? However, we must also consider how it appears in a set-free environment if we openly display our hang-ups or addictions without making any effort to overcome them.

Would others perceive us as dedicated disciples on the path to transformation, or would it create confusion and doubt in their own lives, questioning the effectiveness of the Keys to Being Set Free curriculum?

If they don't see any positive changes in our lives and perceive our involvement as merely a religious gesture, then it is important for us to reconsider and be honest with ourselves before God. Maybe you need to go through the curriculum again with your coach and keep going through it until you find true freedom.

Real transformation is possible, but it requires a genuine commitment to a daily walk in the Spirit. Sometimes change takes time, but there should always be an effort to draw closer to God each day.

Let's not deceive ourselves or the person we are coaching. This is why having a coach in our lives is vital; it provides accountability and guidance. It is also crucial for us to be part of a healthy, Bible-believing church.

WHAT ARE THE RESPONSIBILITIES AND ROLES OF A COACH?

The responsibilities and roles of a Coach are similar to those of a Spiritual advisor or sponsor. As previously mentioned, to have an influence on someone's life, you must be on your own path to freedom.

A coach always directs their student back to Jesus. They do not take ownership of their student but instead work with them as equals, seeking guidance from God in every situation. Every circumstance we face is an opportunity for us to bring Glory to God. Help your student see everything from God's eyes and work together to meditate on God's truth and not the negative circumstances.

- A coach is a prayer warrior and goes the extra mile with their students. They serve as a positive influence, sometimes acting as a counselor and advisor. Regardless of the circumstances, they never condemn their students but lift them up above themselves.

- A coach is open and vulnerable with their student, demonstrating a passion for God's word. They understand that living a life of freedom is impossible without the daily empowerment of the Holy Spirit.

· A coach must be flexible with their time and available to their students during difficult times. Unlearning bad habits can be challenging, especially in the initial transformation period where there will be many up and down moments.

· A coach understands that they need to be patient with their students and recognizes that some may take longer than others to unlearn bad habits. They should never give up on them if they are actively working towards being set free. Jesus persistently demonstrated patience and long-suffering in the nurturing of His disciples, understanding that achieving spiritual growth and true learning requires time.

For instance, as recorded in Mark 8:17-18, Jesus shows frustration, yet patient instruction, when His disciples fail to grasp His teachings, *"Why are you talking about having no bread? Do you still not see or understand? Are your hearts hardened? Do you have eyes but fail to see, and ears but fail to hear?"*

Furthermore, in Matthew 17:17, He calls them an *"unbelieving and perverse generation,"* speaking with a hint of disappointment, while still maintaining a steadfast spirit of mentorship. He repeats His teachings, provides them with experiences for better understanding, and even prays for them further showing His unwavering patience.

His actions embody the verse in *2 Peter 3:9, "The Lord is not slow in keeping his promise, as some understand slowness. Instead, he is patient with you, not wanting anyone to perish, but everyone to come to repentance."* It manifests His intricate understanding that true discipleship is a gradual process.

WHAT MAKES A GOOD COACH?

A coach needs to maintain balance and ensure they are spiritually moving forward in their walk with God before helping someone else on their journey. While it may not be possible to be available all the time, individuals with hang-ups or addictions need a coach's support, especially in the early stages of transformation.

Understanding your role, its significance, and the time and risks that will be involved. Remember, this is a calling, and you are doing this out of obedience to God. You have an obsession with multiplication and witnessing God's kingdom advancing, one disciple at a time.

Relying on the guidance of the Holy Spirit and not coaching someone while being influenced by earthly desires.

Being accountable to another coach and always being available to them.

Caring deeply about your students and desiring their success in becoming a spiritually fulfilled child of God.

GENERAL DO'S AND DON'TS

Some do's and don'ts that coaches should apply in the relationship which are mostly unspoken. They can include the following:

- Coaches should be of the same sex to be most effective unless you are walking a husband and wife through or your spouse is involved if it is someone of the opposite sex.

- Find someone else to support the person with a hang-up or addiction if it is not possible to be available because you are out of town.

- Do not unburden yourself onto the student. You do that in your prayer closet, not out loud in public. If you're working out your salvation in an area you're stuck in, speak with your coach and together bring it before the Lord. But never share your grievances or negativity with your students when it is bringing attention to yourself or how you feel about something.

COACHES BUILD TEAMS

To build a team of Disciples is an answer to the call God gave every believer in Mathew 28:19. Every follower of Christ should be in the business of making disciples. By building a team of disciple warriors you can build a personal discipleship empire for Jesus. A coach is obsessed with multiplication and builds their team so that each of their disciples is multiplying and building their own teams. That is how a movement of God begins, one disciple at a time.

A coach is always mindful that God is always at work around you. We all struggle with hang-ups and or addictions, and some of us are in tremendous pain that needs to be set free. Always be mindful that God can and will lead (FAT) a Faithful, Available, and Teachable person into your life.

There are many people at the end of their rope that are desperately hanging on, as well as many who have found their faith to be stale and need revival themselves.

Keys to Being Set Free is a powerful tool to help broken people find freedom and purpose in their lives.

Don't ever stop being available to what God is asking of you.

Once you have completed the "Keys to Being Set Free" and or "9 Steps Curriculum", Natural Discipleship provides two more curricula to assist you in forming a discipleship leadership team and putting yourself in a position so a Movement of God can happen. We strongly suggest that you go through both of these with your coach, to better equip yourself in leading your team through them.

We can't wait to hear all that God is going to do in your ministry, please keep us informed by sharing your stories with us at www.naturaldiscipleship.com/transfrom

HOW DO I GET STARTED WITH MY NEW STUDENT?

First, ensure your student is (FAT) Faithful, Available, and Teachable. Are they truly prepared for this next phase in their life? Do they understand that they are required to complete the "Keys to Being Set Free" Curriculum and disciple someone else while they are being discipled by you?

It is important to mention that not everyone is ready for a lifestyle of discipleship, so this may not be suitable for everyone. If individuals are truly humble and prepared, you will need to guide them on either purchasing the book "Keys To Being Set Free" online, downloading the free Natural Discipleship app, or printing out the PDF version of the "Keys to Being Set Free" curriculum that can be found in the app.

- They should read the introduction section and inform you if and when they are ready to begin. Schedule your first meeting, determine the day and time, and have them read through Key 1, answering all the associated questions before your meeting.

- Ensure that they complete the assigned work of the next key before you meet each week. If you cannot finish a Key, mark your progress and resume from where you left off during the next meeting. Always allow room for the Holy Spirit to guide your conversations.

- Make prayer a priority in every meeting, always open and close with prayer, and pray anytime during your meeting as the Lord leads.

Natural Discipleship
10524 Moss Park Rd #204-339
Orlando Fl, 32832

For further resources and the available app for download go to:
www.naturaldiscipleship.com

For questions, please email us at: info@naturaldiscipleship.com

Experience Even More

Natural Discipleship

provides an app that offers the tools and resources needed to help people have a personal multiplication discipleship ministry.

Download The App

AVAILABLE IN THE APP STORE NOW!

Experience Even More

Natural DISCIPLESHIP
a Be Mission Minded Ministry

Natural Discipleship offers four curriculum resources that are essential in assisting you with your personal discipleship ministry focused on multiplication.

- The 9-Step Multiplication
- The Discover the Keys to Being Set Free
- The 5 Keys to Building a Leadership team
- The 5 Keys to leading a Spiritual Movement

Start your personal discipleship ministry focused on multiplication today!

www.naturaldiscipleship.com

9-Step Multiplication
CURRICULUM

5 Keys to Leading a Spiritual Movement
CURRICULUM

Keys to Being Set Free
CURRICULUM

5 Keys to Building A Leadership Team
CURRICULUM

PERSONAL NOTES

PERSONAL NOTES

PERSONAL NOTES

PERSONAL NOTES

www.ingramcontent.com/pod-product-compliance
Lightning Source LLC
Chambersburg PA
CBHW041136120626
46547CB00020B/3012